D0053504

3

Freud

a biographical introduction

Freud

a biographical introduction

Penelope Balogh

Charles Scribner's Sons
New York

W

To my students, who forced me to think again.
I would like to remind them of Freud's statement, 'I have assuredly not dug up more than a fragment of the truth'.

The front cover illustration is based on Oscar Nemon's sculpture of Freud, unveiled in 1970, which stands outside the Hampstead Library in London.

Copyright © 1971 Penelope Balogh

A-1.72 [c]

Printed in the United States of America
Library of Congress Catalog Card Number 70-174649
SBN 684-12669-9 (trade cloth)
SBN 684-12670-2 (trade paper)

Contents

Preface

Until Freud published *Studies on Hysteria* in 1895, the idea that there was an unconscious part of the human mind attracted only the occasional philosopher and poet. Scientists spent no time considering such a concept; indeed the possibility that, hidden in each individual, there lies a completely unknown, unknowable part of the mind, was first considered highly offensive, especially as Freud pointed out that it was this 'unconscious' which contained the primitive drives of sex and aggression.

Nowadays, when most thinking people have come to take the unconscious for granted, it is strange to contemplate a situation where this idea was new and shocking. The change, in only about half a century, from distaste and disgust to acceptance is one of the most remarkable things about the history of psychoanalysis. Success was due, in the first place, to the fact that Freud himself was a brilliant expositor, and courageous and persevering in following through his discovery. His scientific integrity and his artistic zeal enabled him to test, by himself, all the main implications of psychoanalytic theory, with the result that by the 1920s psychoanalysis had satisfied a small but significant proportion of the medical world in Europe and America.

In reading the story of Freud's life, we may feel that he was a human being like ourselves; that he was someone who not only respected scientific integrity but enjoyed philosophical speculation and romantic drama, someone who at one time was in despair for humanity, and at another time able to admire it. Nevertheless, we should also remember that a person able to throw light for the first time upon the meaning of the strange clues left by the unconscious mind among the welter of material from the conscious mind must, *ipso facto*, be quite extraordinary. His intellectual voyage of discovery must be likened to those

7

of the first unknown explorers who made little boats and ventured forth on high seas. Like them, he could not at first be sure of his craft, and had to learn how to handle it in different ways and in different weathers; yet unlike them he had no stars, studied first from the safety of the land, by which to navigate during his time at sea. This makes all the more astonishing the magnitude of the revolution in thinking which he achieved through his dedication, genius and courage.

Readers who are not familiar with Freudian terminology will find a brief explanation in the appendix.

I am particularly indebted to Mrs Ernest Jones, who gave me considerable help with regard to proper sequence, facts and spelling. I should also like to take this opportunity to express my great debt to her husband's biography of Freud. It will be obvious to those who know this work, and the shortened version made by Lionel Trilling and Steven Marcus, that I have used both freely for much essential information.

1 The early years

Freud was born[1] on the evening of 6 May, 1856 in Freiberg, Moravia, which was then part of the Austro-Hungarian Empire, but is now in Czechoslovakia.

His parents were Jewish. His father, Jakob, was a wool merchant. He was a widower of forty, with two grown-up sons, when in 1855 he married Freud's mother, a girl twenty years younger than himself. At the time of Freud's birth one of his half-brothers was already married and had a son. This must have set a complicated family pattern for the two boys, one of whom was later on to study with such interest family hierarchies and family interactions and the violent feelings which these can generate.

As the beloved eldest child of a lively and affectionate mother, he gained a self-confidence which stood him in good stead from early days onwards. However, he had many of the experiences to which young children react with shock and upset. Before he was a year old he was presented with a baby brother, and before he reached twenty months that baby had died. When he was two and a half his nurse was dismissed for stealing. She had frequently taken him into a Roman Catholic church, from which he learnt enough of the ideas of heaven and hell, salvation and resurrection to return home and pretend to preach about them. It was in his first home that he remembered being ordered out of his parents' bedroom. There he boasted to his father, who had reproved him for wetting his bed, 'Don't worry, Papa, I'll buy you a beautiful new red bed in Neutitschein' [the district's chief town].

Freud was never able to recall the occasion when he had stitches on his lower jaw for a cut which he got from slipping off a stool when he was two, but he remembered clearly when he was four the experience of seeing his mother naked.

[1] The young Sigmund was born in a caul, emerging with his head still wrapped in a fine membrane.

He played all the usual little boys' games with his nephew John, who was only a year older than himself, and it is more than likely that this companionship laid the foundations of the strong feelings of love and hate which could so often be seen in his friendships with men when he was grown up. It must have been puzzling to play with someone older and stronger who yet addressed your own father as 'grandfather'. Freud himself indicated many years later how his ambivalence towards John had 'conditioned his character'. He wrote that, 'This childish relationship determined my feelings in intercourse with persons of my own age'; and that, 'An intimate friend and a hated enemy have always been indispensable to my emotional life'. He also recalled that he and John used to tease his niece Pauline, John's sister, and since she attracted him very much this memory provided him with further evidence of the interchange and link between erotic feelings and aggression. Freud's sister Anna was born when he was two and a half. He never liked her much, though he felt real affection for the next two sisters, Rosa and Dolfi.

Freiberg had a population of 5000, almost all of whom were Roman Catholics: only two per cent were Protestant and two per cent Jews. By 1859 inflation had increased the poverty of the town, which was largely dependent on textile manufacture. The Czech clothmakers began to blame the Jewish merchants for their plight, and Jakob Freud decided to live and work elsewhere. The family went first to Leipzig, where they stayed for a year. The train taking them away from Freiberg passed through Breslau, where Freud saw gas-jets for the first time; they made him think of 'souls burning in hell'. (Much later, between 1887 and 1899 in the course of his self-analysis, he had a phobia of travelling by train, and was only able to dispel it by connecting it with the fear of losing his home and his mother's care.) A year later the family moved from Leipzig to Vienna. Freud's half-brothers, his sister-in-law and John and Pauline also left Leipzig, but they went to England to live in Manchester. It seems that Freud never ceased to envy them their migration, and England always remained for him the country of his preference.

As Freud says in *The Interpretation of Dreams*, much of

his childhood came back to him during the self-analysis which he began systematically in 1897. Of the years between three and seven he wrote, 'They were hard times – not worth remembering.' According to his own theory (that the human mind represses unpleasant or shocking experiences) we can assume that the early years in Vienna must indeed have been hard. Four incidents that took place then are recorded. Freud could remember consoling his mother when he had made a chair dirty, by promising that he would grow into a great man and buy her another. This, like the story of the red bed, indicates a tendency to restore or repair, and demonstrates how in this boy love was stronger than aggression.

The next memory was of his father's handing him and his sister a book with the suggestion that they should tear out the pictures. Freud traced to this incident his passion for collecting and possessing books.

When he was six his mother assured him that all men were made of earth and so must return to earth. He did not believe this, and to prove it she rubbed her hands together and showed him the dark fragments of epidermis that peeled off. He was amazed, and from then onwards (as he put it much later), 'slowly acquiesced in the idea that I heard expressed elsewhere when I was older: "Thou owest nature a death".'

He could remember once deliberately urinating in his parents' bedroom and being reprimanded by his father, who exclaimed, 'That boy will never amount to anything!', although usually he was extremely proud of the young Sigmund. Allusions to this scene occurred quite often in Freud's adult dreams, together with enumerations of all his accomplishments and successes – the timeless unconscious still needing to prove itself to the father, the first of all important critics, and the symbol of the establishment of society and human achievement.

In 1875 the family moved to a larger flat consisting of five rooms and a 'cabinet' which was allotted to Freud. It was a long, narrow room with a window looking out on to the street, and had just enough space for a bed, a chair or two, a shelf and a writing-desk. Here he lived and worked during his years at school and university, until he became an intern at the hospital. The only change in the room was the increasing number of crowded bookcases. During his teens he even ate his supper there so as to lose no time from studying. Here, too, he always took his friends for serious discussions. The whole household was subordinated to Sigmund's needs and studies, as is shown by the fact that the piano was removed on his insistence because he could not tolerate the noise of his sister's practising. There seems no doubt that his well-known aversion to music was tied up with dislike of competition and the rivalry with siblings.

The atmosphere of Freud's home must have been a great deal more permissive than was general in those days among the middle classes. An example of this was the 'family council', which was a form of consultation between parents and children. All the same, Jakob was a Jewish patriarch, and demanded proper respect. There is a story of how Moritz Rosenthal, the pianist, was once seen arguing in the street with his father. Jakob laughingly reproved the boy. 'What, contradicting your father? My Sigmund's little toe is cleverer than my head, but he would never dare to contradict me!'

Of Freud's religious background we can only make surmises. It looks as if the influence of the Roman Catholic nanny contributed to his antipathy to Christian beliefs and ceremonies. He was certainly conversant with all Jewish customs and festivals, but Jakob Freud was thought of by the family as a free-thinker, and was undoubtedly a liberal-minded man of progressive views. Nevertheless, when Freud was thirty-five his father sent him the family Bible, inscribed to him in Hebrew, with a quotation advising him to read it. Although Freud brought a completely scientific outlook to bear on religious matters, and was more of an atheist than an agnostic, he was always fascinated by religious beliefs, their possible origins, and the mental mechanisms which sustain them. He made few friends who were not Jews, and felt himself to be Jewish to the core, although he had not many noticeable Jewish characteristics, save the usual sensitivity to any hint of anti-Semitism, and a great liking for Jewish jokes and anecdotes. Vienna was, in those days, pervaded by anti-Semitism, and disappointment at his father's passivity in the face of a Gentile's hostility to him in the street was very great. He could not bear it that his father had stepped off the pavement, as he had been ordered to do, and had stooped to pick up his fur hat which the Gentile had knocked off.

Both parents had a hand in giving him his first lessons before he was sent to a private school. At nine he passed into the high school a year earlier than was usual. For the last six of the eight years he was there he was top of his class, and he left with the distinction *summa cum laude*. He learned Greek, Latin and Hebrew, and taught himself Italian and Spanish after he had learned to speak French and English fluently. He began reading Shakespeare at the age of eight, and later often quoted from the plays.

When he was nineteen he went to England to stay with his half-brother Emmanuel – the reward for his excellent record at school – but we know little about the visit. We are told that he envied the relative freedom from persecution which Jews enjoyed in England, and that he learnt to admire Oliver Cromwell, after whom, in due course, he named one of his sons. He impressed Emmanuel most favourably, and later on he confessed that he used to indulge in the fantasy that he was really Emmanuel's son, thinking that if he were his life would be easier.

Freud seems to have fallen in love only once before he met his wife. This was when he revisited his birthplace, Freiberg, and stayed with the Fluss family, who had been friends of his parents. Their daughter Gisela had been a childhood companion, and he fell in love with her at once. He was far too shy to talk to her, let alone say what he felt, and after a few days she had to go off to school, leaving Freud to wander in the woods wishing that his family had never gone to Vienna but had stayed near Freiberg, where he could have grown up into a stout country lad and married Gisela.

He was left entirely free to decide his own career on leaving school; but a middle-class Viennese Jew had only industry, business, law or medicine to choose from. Freud's childhood dreams of becoming a great general or Minister of State soon vanished under the impact of this reality. In a letter written much later, he admitted that it

13

was Goethe's beautiful essay on nature, which he had heard read aloud at a popular lecture, that led him to decide to study medicine. This essay is a romantic picture of Nature as a bountiful mother allowing her favourite children to explore her secrets. Freud was fully aware of his privileged position, both within his own family and as a gifted intellectual in the student world. Yet all sorts of proofs are sought for by adolescents to reassure themselves of their worth, and so it was Goethe's reiteration of a happy theme which provided reassurance for Freud. He often said how little he felt himself to be identified with the profession of physician, but that curiosity about human beings, and reverence for scientific observation, led him to medical research. The incentive to understand more about mankind was further stimulated by the work of Charles Darwin, which excited all educated people in Europe during the 1870s.

It is thought that, just because he was so attracted to philosophical speculation, he chose to read very little philosophy during his early student days, thus unconsciously checking his bent towards making abstractions and instead forcing himself to remain concerned with concrete, scientific data. His balance and scope are illustrated by his ability to be orderly and thorough in organizing a whole mass of facts into a systematic group (well instanced in *The Interpretation of Dreams*), yet it must be noted as well that he hated to feel fettered by precise definitions. Once when asked why he had used some ambiguous or unclear phrase he shrugged his shoulders with a grimace and answered 'pure *schlamperei*' (sloppiness). These aspects of Freud's mentality – his longing to think and write freely and speculatively, and his simultaneous concern for objectivity and proof – illustrate the duality of function which he later observed as existing in every part of life.

Freud became a medical student at the age of seventeen, but he took three years longer than usual to complete the course. He immersed himself in the studies that intrigued him, and was somewhat negligent of those proper to the medical career itself. In his first term he signed up for twelve lectures in anatomy and six in chemistry, with five hours of practical work per week. In the summer, botany, microscopy and mineralogy were added, plus a course on biology and Darwinism, and one on 'The Physiology of Voice and Speech' by the famous German physiologist Brücke, who was later to become very important to him.

The next year was spent on anatomical dissection, physics, physiology, and zoology; once a week he went to a philosophy seminar, although philosophy by 1872 was no longer compulsory for medical students. In his fourth term he struck out even more independently, attending zoology lectures other than those specially arranged for medical students. Later he added another course on Aristotle's logic, and eleven hours a week of physiology lectures by Brücke.

In the summer of 1876, after two and a half years at the university, Freud was sufficiently distinguished as a student to be given a research grant at the newly founded Experimental Station for Marine Zoology at Trieste. His task was to try to clarify the structure of the sex glands of eels, a mystery which had puzzled scientists for centuries. 'No one,' he wrote, 'has ever found a mature male eel – no one has yet seen the testes of the eel.' Clearly this is somehow bound up with the astonishing migration of eels, which takes place before mating. Having dissected some four hundred eels, Freud found in many of them a small-lobed organ which Syrski in 1874 had considered to be the testes. Microscopic examination pointed towards confirmation that it might well be an immature testicular organ, but no definite evidence could be adduced. Subsequent papers followed Freud's and agreed with him, but at the time the ambitious student must have been dissatisfied with such inconclusive results, for even then, like anyone else, he had hoped for an immediate and brilliant discovery.

By the end of his third year Freud realized that his gifts had 'peculiarities and limitations', and that success would never be his in many of the departments of science into which 'youthful eagerness' had plunged him. He quoted Mephistopheles' warning: 'It is in vain that you range round from science to science; each man learns only what he can.'

Nevertheless, in Ernst Brücke's physiology laboratory he found 'rest and satisfaction', and men whom he could respect and take as models – not only Brücke but his assistants, Exner and Fleischl-Marxow, too. Brücke had a formidable reputation as a brilliant, dedicated scientist, and Freud wrote that the image of the 'terrible gaze' of his steel-blue eyes, fixed on him on one occasion when he was late, afterwards returned to him at all sorts of moments when he was tempted to do anything in a slipshod fashion. Here he was substituting for his permissive family a more exacting and intellectual 'father figure', using this image to drive himself on to perfection. Nevertheless, the fact of being tied down to precise measurement curbed his natural boldness and imagination, and for ten years his obedience to a pedantic form of reasoning influenced and inhibited his more poetical flights of thought.

In Brücke's Institute Freud was inspired by the concept, completely adhered to then by some of the most brilliant scientists of the day, 'that human beings, like all living things, were explicable in physical-chemical terms and in those terms only'.

The principle of the conservation of energy – the idea that the sum of forces remains constant in every isolated system, that progress in knowledge reduces these forces to two, *attraction* and *repulsion*, and that this theory is equally applicable to the organism Man – is written into the two volumes of Brücke's published lectures. Here is presented most of what was known at that time about the transformation and interplay of physical forces in the living organism. Freud's description of the dynamic aspect of psychoanalysis corresponds closely to Brücke. In 1926 he wrote, 'The forces assist or inhibit one another, combine with one another, enter into compromise with one another, etc.' There is no doubt that Brücke's influence on Freud had a permanent effect – not only the link with Darwinian studies, which work in this Institute provided, but Brücke's personality, exacting, forceful, free from vanity or lust for power, must have set a pattern for Freud which was of more importance to him emotionally than that of any other teacher or colleague. It also demanded of him a worship of intellectual integrity, a deep reverence for the truth as far as he could see it.

It was in Brücke's Institute that Freud was set to work

with a microscope to investigate the histology of nerve cells. At the time there was much controversy as to whether the nervous system of higher animals was different in kind from that of lower forms of life. Freud established that cells, discovered by Reissner in the fish Petromyzon, of the genus Cyclostomatae, were nothing but spiral ganglion cells which, in their scattered way, marked an evolutionary path. This solution was a triumph of precision and genetic interpretation – one of a thousand such small steps towards establishing among scientists the conviction of the unity of all organisms. It contributed conclusively to the theory that the cells of the nervous system of lower animals show a continuity with those of higher animals and that there is no sharp distinction.

Next Freud examined the nerve cells of crayfish. Here he established that the ganglion consists of two substances; but although at this point he was actually dealing with the very material which later led to the establishment of the famous neurone theory (the basis of modern neurology) the discipline and caution for which his laboratory research was noticeable restrained his imagination in this field. He did not allow himself to take the next step. This is very interesting, in the light of the boldness and imagination shown in his later thinking. But he was inventive enough to modify the Reichart formula – a mixture of nitric acid and glycerine used for preparing nervous tissue for the microscope – and later on he employed gold chloride for staining nervous tissue. He must have been an expert technician, for he speaks of studying nerve tissue in the crayfish *in vivo*, and he himself drew the illustrations for his publication on the Petromyzon.

In the course of such work Freud came to see that progress in knowledge first needs new or improved methods, and next an organization of both the new and the old knowledge into a working theory. Thence theory can lead to speculation. It is very rare for one and the same man to be successful in all three phases of research, yet Freud, when working on the theory and practice of psychoanalysis, was equally adept at all. As an experimental neurologist he adhered to anatomy, and the microscope was his only tool – in this field the follower rather than the leader was uppermost. The same thing was true of the first work which he did of his own accord with neurotic patients. Early on he decided against the interference of hypnosis and electrical stimulation; instead of leading his patients he chose to look and to listen to them in a new way, following them, as it were. Never before had patients been treated like this. He was confident that if he could perceive the structure of a neurosis he would eventually understand it, and find power over the forces that had brought it about. It is important to remember that this basically passive attitude, one of careful observation and study, is the precursor of all his later active therapeutic procedure, including the interpretations and explanations which are inevitably the second part of psychoanalytic treatment.

Meanwhile, in 1879 he began his military service. In those days medical students could still live at home during this time, and the greater part of their duties consisted of standing about in hospitals. Freud coped with his boredom during this period by translating a book by John Stuart Mill – the first of five long books which he translated.[1] Three of the essays in this book concerned problems of labour, the enfranchisement of women, and socialism. A fourth contained Mill's sympathetic treatment of Plato's theory of reminiscence, some of which, many years later, Freud wove into his own book, *Beyond the Pleasure Principle*.

But most of these years, of course, were filled with orthodox medical studies. He learned from several world-famous specialists who gave him more than routine knowledge, being innovators in their own fields – Hebra in dermatology, Arlt in ophthalmology, and Billroth in surgery – yet the only lectures he admitted to finding really interesting were Meynert's on psychiatry.

Freud passed his final examination with the grade 'excellent' in March 1881. He attributed this result entirely to his photographic memory, which enabled him to reproduce parts of text-books which he had skimmed through merely once, in the greatest haste, during his short

[1] He used an unusual method; he would read a passage, close the book and consider how a German writer would express the same material. Then he would write it.

18

period of revision. Qualification made little difference to his way of life; he went on working in the Brücke Institute, engaged on work which could be thought of as one day leading to a chair in physiology. Greatly preferring research to medical practice, he divided his time between demonstrating in physiology and making investigations into the analysis of gases.

He described 1882 as 'the gloomiest and least successful year of my professional life', for the work on which he was engaged neither advanced him in his career nor improved his precarious financial situation. In view of his need to earn more money Brücke advised him to abandon a theoretical career. Up till then his father, now sixty-seven and still with a young family to rear, had kept him, for his university grant amounted to approximately £8 a year and his publications earned him little more. Nevertheless, he might well have rejected Brücke's counsel had he not by then already fallen in love with his future wife, Martha Bernays, to whom he became engaged in June, 1882. This forced him to realize that a career in scientific research was out of the question, since he had no private income and there were too many men senior to him in his beloved laboratory. So, at the age of twenty-six, he entered the General Hospital in Vienna.

Freud spent two years living and studying in the hospital. In those days medical students on the continent were not given practical experience during their training. After two months in the surgical wards he entered Professor Nothnagel's clinic as 'aspirant'. Professor Nothnagel was known to be strict – 'anyone who needs more than five hours' sleep should not study medicine' – but nevertheless all the students idolized him. Freud, however, became more and more convinced that he was not a born doctor, and he found little interest either in treating sick patients or in studying the physical aspect of their diseases.

In May 1883 he transferred to Meynert's psychiatric clinic, where he was at once appointed *Sekundararzt* (resident house physician). So, at the age of twenty-seven, he left home, never to sleep there again. He served in the clinic for five months, two of them in the male wards, three in the female, and soon became popular among his colleagues. He found Meynert 'more stimulating than a host of friends', and seven hours daily in the wards 'hardly sufficient to cover the ground'. Meynert was generally regarded as the greatest brain anatomist of that time, an opinion with which Freud concurred. Studying the disorder then called 'Meynert's amentia' (acute hallucinatory psychosis) he obtained vivid impressions of the wish-fulfilment mechanism, and his observations at this time must have been helpful to him later when he began his investigations of the unconscious.

In October he moved to the department of dermatology. There he gained the experience which he needed in cases of syphilis, with its connexion with diseases of the nervous system. Early the following year he went on to the department for nervous diseases. When two of the doctors were called away to help with a cholera epidemic on the Austro-Montenegrin borders, he was given the responsible position of superintendent with full charge of 106 patients, ten nurses and three doctors.

In September 1885 he was made *Privatdozent* – a term which has no counterpart in Anglo-Saxon medical establishments. For Freud it involved writing a thesis on the anatomy of the medulla, and of being examined orally by three professors. He also had to give a public lecture, and a formal clearance of his character with police headquarters was required.

For a time he went back to the ophthalmology and dermatology departments, though in a considerably senior position, and for part of 1885 he worked in a private mental hospital in Oberdöbling, outside Vienna. During this period he had applied for a much-prized travelling grant, and was successful despite tremendous competition. Many of the eminent professors for whom he had worked, most especially Brücke, had supported his application. So at the end of August 1885, at the age of twenty-nine, he left the General Hospital for good, having worked there for three years. During that period he had completed research on the medulla and had been recognized as a *Dozent* in neurology; now he was on his way to Paris to work under Charcot, then at the height of his fame as a specialist in nervous diseases.

2 Cocaine – betrothal – marriage

No life of Freud is complete without some reference to his early work on cocaine.

An autobiographical note reveals his genuine disappointment at having so narrowly missed being known as the discoverer of its anaesthetic properties. He describes how in 1884 he obtained some of the little known alkaloid cocaine in order to study its physiological action. In the middle of this research he accepted an opportunity to go and stay near his fiancée, Martha Bernays, whom he had not seen for two years. Thus he contented himself with a short monograph on the subject, prophesying that further uses for cocaine would soon be found. At the same time he suggested to an ophthalmologist, Leopold Königstein, that he should investigate how far cocaine could be used as an anaesthetic in treating and operating on diseases of the eye. On his return he found that another less intimate friend, Carl Koller, had made decisive experiments which he had already demonstrated at a congress. It was Koller, therefore, who was recognized as the discoverer of local anaesthesia by cocaine, now so important in minor surgery.

Freud had decided to take cocaine himself after reading that it had been used to increase the stamina of soldiers. He found that it changed his mood from depression to elation, and recommended it to his brilliant friend, Fleischl-Marxow, who had become a morphia addict after operations on his right hand which had left him in great pain. Through the use of cocaine this friend was weaned from his morphia addiction within a few days, but it was about two years before Freud and others recognized that cocaine could also become an addiction. By then (1887) cocaine addicts were having to be treated all over Europe, and it was referred to as 'the third scourge of humanity'. However, before that Freud and all his circle had experimented with it for many different ailments, from

21

sea-sickness to trigeminal neuralgia. Freud's essay on the subject demonstrated a flight from all the rest of his sober scientific presentations. It included phrases like 'the most gorgeous excitement' which he said was displayed by animals after an injection, and he used the expression 'an offering' instead of a dose.

It is hard to say how greatly his enthusiasm for cocaine, during a period when its properties were not yet established, damaged his reputation and was remembered against him when he later challenged the medical world. What is certain is that Freud – like all very original men – was a complete mixture of ardent, almost reckless single-mindedness and cautious, careful checking and re-checking. Unfortunately there seems to be no comprehensive written description of any of his other early ideas, save those referring to the gold chloride method of staining nervous tissue.

The way in which a person responds to the experience of falling in love, and his relationship with the beloved, is always most revealing.

Freud first met Martha one evening in April 1882. Returning home from work he was arrested by the sight of a slim, pale girl gaily chatting away and peeling an apple. To the general surprise of his family, he joined them instead of rushing to his room. Since his schoolboy fantasies about Gisela Fluss ten years before, Freud had remained almost totally absorbed by work. Decades later he wrote to one correspondent, concerning the subject of greater freedom for youth in the sphere of sex, that 'I myself availed myself but little of it'.

In the days that followed their first meeting, Freud was able to present only a rather unsociable and eccentric exterior, but as he became aware of the seriousness of his feelings he realized that he must declare himself, 'because any suggestion of artificiality towards such a girl would be unbearable'. He sent her a red rose every day, each accompanied by a motto on a visiting card in Latin, Spanish, English or German. His favourite name for her, 'Princess', came from likening her to the fairy from whose lips fell roses and pearls.

Her brother Eli – who acted as head of the family since their father was dead – advised her against marrying someone much older than herself, saying that it was foolish to marry unless one was really in love, but two months after their first meeting they became engaged. Martha had given him a ring of her father's some time before, yet it took Freud many months to give up the idea that he had been the only one in love at their betrothal, and he was fiercely jealous of her other admirers. Among them were Max Mayer, a musician, and Fritz Wahle, a painter. He wrote, 'I think there is general enmity between artists and those engaged in the details of scientific work. We know that they possess in their art a master key to open with ease all female hearts, whereas we stand helpless at the strange design of the lock and have first to torment ourselves to discover a suitable key.' Eventually Freud realized that Wahle was in love with Martha without conscious knowledge of the fact, and that he was accepted by her only as an intimate friend; and in his understanding of the situation he shows a wisdom that foreshadows the future leader of a future psychology. After a quarrel he wrote of Fritz, 'The man who brings tears to my eyes must do a great deal before I forgive him – I am made of harder stuff than he is – he will find he is not my equal', and, *Only in logic are contradictions unable to co-exist; in feelings they are able to continue alongside each other quite happily'*. But his jealousy and despair, while he still felt that Fritz could succeed in persuading Martha to jilt him were very great indeed; and his distrust and hatred of a man whom in other circumstances he could well have liked left an unforgettable and painful memory.

Other emotional experiences also helped him to understand the entanglements and frictions that exist between human beings who are deeply involved with each other and within families. Martha's family were orthodox Jews: her grandfather, Isaac Bernays, had been Chief Rabbi of Hamburg and was related to the poet Heine. Her mother was particularly strict in her observance of the faith, and in order not to write a letter with pen and ink on the Sabbath Martha would compose one in pencil in the garden! Freud was greatly annoyed at what he called her

23

weakness in not standing up to her mother. He disliked his future mother-in-law's complacency and her love of comfort, which clashed with his preference for threshing matters out, however painful. He disapproved, also, of her refusal to resign herself to her age or to put the children's interests first, as his own mother did. When Freud realized that Minna, Martha's sister, was not so obedient or respectful to her mother, he wrote to his beloved with clear-sighted acumen, 'You don't really love her very much and so are as considerate to her as possible; Minna loves her, but doesn't spare her'.

On another occasion, when there was a dispute between the two families, Freud stated that he would actually have broken with her had she not sided with him. Here is evidence of a youthful immaturity which perhaps he never outgrew, for it seems that he found it impossible to tolerate having someone close to him who thought differently. However, six months after Martha and Freud had become engaged, Eli, Martha's brother, announced his engagement to Freud's oldest sister; and although Frau Bernays remained unreconciled to Martha's choice of suitor the two families resumed relations. Later on, hostility broke out once more, always beginning with Freud expressing criticism of his brother-in-law; but by 1892 we hear of him helping Eli to emigrate to the United States and even keeping his daughter, Lucie, for a year with his own children until she could follow her parents.

Freud wrote over 900 letters to his fiancée, for they were separated for at least three of the four years of their engagement. One letter demonstrates Freud's ever-present candour when replying to a self-deprecatory remark of Martha's, 'I know you are not beautiful in a painter's or sculptor's sense; if you insist on strict correctness in the use of words then I must confess you are not beautiful. But I was not flattering you in what I said. I cannot flatter; I can, it is true, be mistaken. What I meant to convey was how much the magic of your being expresses itself in your countenance and your body, how much there is visible in your appearance that reveals how sweet, generous and reasonable you are.'

During this long engagement Freud's demands on

24

Martha might well have made someone less loyal leave him. He did his best to stop her 'trying to be on good terms with everyone', and insisted that she should always side with him against her mother and brother in any quarrel; and, of course, he wanted her to give up her 'religious prejudices'. Most of the time Martha's delaying tactics succeeded, but Freud preferred to have things out in open conflict, so there must have been many difficult moments.

The intensity of his misery when Martha's mother decided to leave Vienna and take her family back to Hamburg in 1883, and his anger at Martha's not putting up a better fight over this issue, filled a month of his letters with bitterness. Her replies are full of bewilderment.

Much later he learned to appreciate Martha's ability not to give in to him on every matter; but during the first part of their engagement his doubt of her love for him, and of his own lovableness, must have compelled him to try and insist on her identifying with him and his views in every matter. His poverty, and the obstacle this made to their getting married, must have been continuously in the forefront of his mind during these years, and his frustration and loneliness when Martha returned with her mother to Hamburg must have been responsible for many of the gloomy, reproachful sentences in some of his letters to her. Violent anger alternated with deep tenderness and affection. However, after a visit to Hamburg in 1885 Freud's ability to tolerate the privation grew, and his resentment at their separation changed into a longing which increased as the hope of fulfilment grew nearer. Thirty years later, when he wrote about the pathological nature of the state of being in love, he may well have remembered writing to Martha, 'One is very crazy when one is in love'. He wrote this at a time when he thought that Martha was lying ill. His letters reveal tremendous and complicated feelings, the heights of bliss, the depths of despair, the most thoughtful tenderness, fierce jealousy.

From reading about these emotional storms during his engagement period, one can see that Freud was not just the calm scientist he is so often depicted as being, but had within him a great intensity of feeling – potent repressions. There were to be several more times when he would be torn by love and hate, but this was the only time in his life when such emotions centred on a woman. Once married, it was totally different: differences of opinion seemed hardly to exist. His promise of 'a quarrel once a week' was forgotten; the only argument recorded was to do with whether mushrooms should be cooked with or without their stalks!

Married quietly by both civil and Jewish law in September 1886, Freud and his wife returned to Vienna and to the practice which Freud had begun. At first he was extremely short of patients, and had to pawn his gold watch. His wedding present to Martha, her gold watch, would have followed, but for timely help from her sister Minna. Then the tide began to turn, and Freud was sure of earning enough to be able to write in 1888, 'We live pretty happily in steadily increasing unassumingness. When we hear the baby laugh we imagine it is the loveliest thing that can happen to us. I am not ambitious, and do not work very hard.' By August 1891 they had two sons and a daughter and, needing more rooms, moved to 19 Berggasse, where they lived for the next forty-seven years. Three more children were born there, a son and two daughters.

Minna Bernays came to live with the family in 1896. Her fiancé, Freud's friend Ignez Schönberg, had died, and she far preferred helping her sister care for the children to any other occupation. She was a witty and interesting person with a pungent tongue and literary interests. She and Freud got on excellently, but the gossip which arose about them because she accompanied Freud on some short holidays when Martha was unable to travel is without foundation.

From his correspondence, the two outstanding impressions that one receives of Freud's life before marriage are of his poverty and of the goodness of his friends. His own family was extremely poor. His father at seventy was almost senile and had never been very successful, and his mother needed to be sent out of Vienna when it was very hot, as she had tuberculosis of the lung. Since several sisters were still at home, making ends meet was difficult, and Freud must have found this a constant source of anxiety in the light of the small amount he could contribute.

26

His attitude to money was neither rigid nor obsessive. He borrowed freely, lent when he could, and was generous. However, he made his daily needs minimal. The expenditure on food and clothes, noted faithfully in letters to Martha during their engagement, was extremely small. Soon after his marriage there was a morning when he had to borrow a coat to visit a patient, his own being in need of so much repair! He regarded money as a commodity to be used to fulfil his needs, and the absence of it as he would any other frustration. He minded not being able to give Martha expensive presents. Once, when he wanted her to have a gold snake bangle, he wrote to her that all *Dozent's* wives wore such bangles to distinguish them from the wives of other doctors!

Foremost among those who stood by him financially must be mentioned his old school teacher, Hammerschlag, of whom he was tremendously fond, and his friend Josef Breuer. The former was himself existing on a small pension, the latter was indubitably well off, an established doctor, and certainly in a position to lend to Freud. Fleischl, who like Freud had studied under Brücke, became a constant stand-by in 1884, but he died before Freud was able to repay him. Josef Paneth, another colleague from the Institute of Physiology, set aside a donation 'to shorten the time of his waiting to marry', and Freud borrowed from this sum to offset some of the cost of his visits to Paris and Berlin. The number and strength of the friendships with which his life was filled testify to the fact – of which he was himself aware – that, though his manners were sometimes brusque on first acquaintance, the more one got to know him the more likeable he became. He said of himself, 'Nature did not give me that indefinite something which immediately attracts people. It has always taken me some time to win a friend, and every time I meet someone I notice that to begin with some impulse leads him to underestimate me. What compensates me for this is the thought of how closely all those who have become my friends keep to me.'

There were really two distinct sets of friends. Those whom Freud got to know through his scientific and medical work were mainly older than himself. The others, known as 'the Band', were contemporaries, about fifteen or twenty in number, who would meet in the Café Kurzwell for cards and chess. Of Freud's older friends, Breuer had the most sympathetic personality. Freud described talking to him as, 'Like sitting in the sun . . . one does not adequately characterize him by saying only good things about him; one has also to emphasize the absence of so much badness'. Later, in the nineties, when Breuer could not agree with him, Freud felt bitter animosity towards him, but he never let this be seen in anything that he published.

While writing of the personal aspects of Freud's life, reference should be made to his physical troubles. In 1882 he suffered an attack of typhoid which left a toxic condition, as did the smallpox which he had in 1885, though the attack in itself was mild. Sciatica, brachial neuritis and rheumatic pains in the back and arms also troubled him. He endured nasal catarrh with sinus complications for years. Recovering in 1882 from a severe angina of the throat which had prevented speech or swallowing for several days, he wrote to Martha of how he was seized with a gigantic hunger and an indescribable longing for her.

From all this, it can be seen that Freud was fully conversant with physical and psychological suffering. Among his psychosomatic symptoms were severe indigestion and constipation. His moodiness never reached what could be termed true depression, but he often lost all capacity to enjoy himself, and felt desperately tired. In those days, before his own work in psychoanalysis, Freud was led to attribute his 'neurasthenia' to the strain of the life he was living, describing as 'a stroke of magic' the sense of well-being as soon as he was with Martha. This led him to think that he would always be well if, after marriage, he lived modestly, giving up his ambition to make discoveries. Despite the bad moods, many of his letters reflect his confidence in eventual success and happiness, and demonstrate also his swift transition from elation to bitterness and despair. Both sexual and economic privations were for him extreme, and thanks to his later work we now know that these provocations usually exaggerate the natural swing of temperament. What must be borne in mind is

28

that he was one of those people who always make a challenge out of life. To be forced to disregard the need to earn properly, as his scientific work demanded; to delay his marriage and ask the same sacrifice of Martha; to spend so much time and energy on his work and therefore of necessity away from her – all this would have taxed anyone's strength of purpose. Freud was tremendously envious of those who could have both a happy private life as well as a successful professional life.

Though she was well-educated and intelligent Martha was not an intellectual, and in later years she found the affairs of everyday life enough to absorb her whole attention. She enjoyed discussing good novels with Freud, and they often quoted poetry to each other, but it seems that he was never able to interest her in any philosophical or scientific writing. Of the temptation of St Anthony he wrote to her, 'With unsurpassable vividness it throws at one's head the whole trashy world; for it calls up not only the great problems of knowledge but the real riddles of life, all the conflicts of feelings and impulses, and confirms the awareness of our perplexity in the mysteriousness that reigns everywhere'. The sense of 'the mysteriousness that reigns everywhere' never left Freud. Perhaps one of the false statements about psychoanalysis which he would now most regret is that its doctrine robs life of its mystery. He was the first to point out that psychoanalysts could be just as mistaken about a fellow human-being as other people, and that it took long study and much listening before analytical knowledge could come to a reliable judgement.

His views about women and their best place being in the home is well expressed in his translation of John Stuart Mill. 'I believe that all reforming action in law and education breaks down in front of the fact that, long before the age at which man can earn a position in society, Nature has determined woman's destiny through beauty, charm and sweetness. Law and custom have much to give women that has been withheld from them, but the position of women will surely be what it is – in youth an adored darling and in mature years a loved wife.'

3 Studies on Hysteria

Brief reference has been made to Freud's visit to Paris in 1885 to study under Charcot, who was to be the most important influence in turning him from neurology to psychopathology. 'No other human being has affected me in such a way,' he wrote to Martha. 'Whether the seed will ever bring forth fruit I do not know.' At his hospital, the Salpêtrière, Charcot demonstrated the very surprising effects of hypnotic suggestion. Here for the first time medical men could witness involuntary physical obedience to mental stimulation. Physical symptoms appeared, and various behavioural responses were evoked, which had nothing to do with physical treatment or medication. Freud attended many of Charcot's demonstrations and lectures, and it was during this period that he began to think about the possible existence of an unconscious mind whose dynamics were completely different from those of conscious thought.

In his letters Freud described Charcot vividly. He contrasted his warm, keen interest in his patients with the 'serene superficiality' of Viennese physicians. The lithograph depicting Charcot which he brought back from Paris shows the great man holding forth to assistants and students, while the patient whose case is under consideration is reclining in a semi-conscious state. Freud's eldest daughter has written of how the picture held a great fascination for her when she was little, and that she could remember the look her father often gave it, which made her realize that it held important memories for him.

At Salpêtrière Freud began by working on the brains of infants and on a descending degeneration in the spinal cord; he also made a detailed report on the findings of an autopsy on a woman who had been in the hospital since 1853 suffering from hemiplegia (paralysis of one side). He showed how her sclerosis resulted from an embolism that had taken place more than thirty years before. This was almost the last of his work with a microscope – henceforth he was to become a pure clinician. He gave seven reasons for coming to this decision. *When there are a multiplicity of reasons or excuses given it usually indicates suppression of a single real and fundamental reason*; so we can guess that he gave up this sort of research because of the fascination for psychopathology which Charcot had stimulated.

Freud also realized that, for him, married life could mean only clinical work, and he wrote at that time to Martha, 'You may be sure that I have overcome my love for science in so far as it came between us'. He had assured her once before that anatomy of the brain was the only serious rival she had ever had or was likely to have.

Freud writes in his own autobiographical study that what impressed him most while he was with Charcot were the investigations into hysteria. The conformity to laws of hysterical phenomena, the frequent occurrence of hysteria in men, the production of hysterical paralyses and contractures by hypnotic suggestion, and the fact that such artificial products showed the same features as spontaneous attacks amazed and at first provoked him, along with other visitors, to scepticism.

Charcot's patience and friendliness in the face of this scepticism must have remained an inspiration to Freud when his own theories were objects of derision and disbelief. A remark which Charcot made during one discussion when his audience expressed grave doubts, 'Ca n'empêche pas d'exister' (That does not stop it from existing), left an indelible mark on Freud's mind.

Freud wanted to make a detailed comparison between hysterical and organic paralyses, and to establish the thesis that in hysterical paralyses and anaesthesias the various parts of the body affected are demarcated according to the popular idea of their limits and *not* according to anatomical facts, that is, according to ideation and not according to the physical fact. Charcot agreed that this was so, but it seemed that he was never really interested in penetrating deeply into the psychology of neuroses; nor did he offer any encouragement when Freud described to him a particularly interesting case in which his friend Breuer had been

31

involved, known as 'Fraulein Anna O.'. Breuer had often discussed this girl's treatment with Freud before he went to Paris. Many of her hysterical symptoms and confusions had been cured by Breuer's daily use of hypnosis, yet she never became completely well.

Freud, who found the laboratory conditions at the Salpêtrière unsatisfactory, returned to Vienna in the spring of 1886, having previously arranged to translate Charcot's book *New Lectures on the Diseases of the Nervous System, Especially on Hysteria*. He spent a few weeks in Berlin on the way in order to learn at Adolf Baginsky's clinic something about the general diseases of children. This gave him further experience for the position which he had been offered in Vienna, that of director of the new neurological department in the first public Institute for Children's Diseases. Freud worked at the institute for many years, spending several hours there three times a week.

The only paper that he published during the next five years was about two cases of hemianopsia (a complaint in which half the field of vision is grossly disturbed), which had occurred in two children of two and three years. Such cases had hitherto been unobserved. His translation of Charcot was published during this period.

In treating his patients – the greater number of whom were neurotic – Freud had at first confined himself to electrotherapy, baths and massage, but in December 1887, and for the next eighteen months, he persevered with hypnotic suggestion. This often brought gratifying success, and replaced his former feeling of helplessness in the face of neurotic symptoms. For a time he had the pleasure of seeming to work magic. A number of his former colleagues were scornful of hypnosis, but this in no way deterred Freud. What did deter him was that sometimes he was not always able to induce hypnosis at all, and quite often not deeply enough for the patient's needs. Also, the patient's symptoms could return.

In the summer of 1889 he went to Nancy with the idea of perfecting his hypnotic technique. There he saw Liébault working among the poor, and was a spectator of Bernheim's experiments with hospital patients. But Bernheim, too, failed to induce somnambulism in one of

Freud's gifted hysterical patients, who had been asked to come to Nancy for treatment since Freud had been able to achieve only temporary success in treating her. Bernheim told Freud frankly that his great therapeutic successes, when he used suggestion, were mainly achieved with hospital inmates, seldom with private patients, i.e., not with more educated people. This reinforced in Freud the realization that the immense hidden forces within the mind required some other mode of release than that obtained through the repetition of monotonous suggestions. At the same time, hypnotism combined with massage, baths and prescribed rest showed him that one of the reasons why many beneficial results were transitory was because the patient, while in contact with the physician, sheds his symptoms to please the physician, but these can return when the contact is withdrawn.

In 1891 Freud's first book, entitled *On Aphasia*, which he dedicated to Breuer, was published. It contained a closely worked-out criticism of the Wernicke-Lichtheim doctrine of aphasia which was universally accepted at that time. This doctrine consisted of schemes of the supposed connexions of centres between the frontal and temporal lobes of the brain, accounting for motor aphasia (disturbance of speech) and sensory aphasia (inability to understand speech). Freud showed up various contradictions from existing published cases, and introduced a functional explanation. In doing so he quoted Hughlings Jackson's theory of 'disinvolution', which held that the more recently acquired and less important capacities suffer sooner than the earlier and more fundamental ones. He also challenged the notion that ideas and memories can be pictured as attached to special brain cells, and protested vigorously against confounding physiological with psychological data. Freud had little luck with this book. Of 850 copies, only 257 were sold in nine years, and the rest were pulped.

In 1891, in collaboration with his friend and colleague Dr Oscar Rie, he published a massive monograph on the unilateral paralyses of children. Thirty-five cases are described in detail, and it is still held by neurologists to be a first-class clinical study. Other papers on cerebral diplegias and paralyses in childhood followed. By the time

33

he was asked to write the section on infantile cerebral paralysis in Nothnagel's *Encyclopaedia of Medicine*, Freud was far more interested in psychopathology: nevertheless his section – which is 327 pages long – was held to be the most thorough and complete exposition yet written.

Ernest Jones dates the end of Freud's active neurological period as coinciding with his obituary notice of Charcot in September 1893. Eventually Freud demonstrated a patient of twenty-nine who after a quarrel with his brother developed hemianaesthesia (anaesthesia of half the body) with disturbances in the visual field and colour sense. This time Freud was applauded but still no further interest was shown in his work, and he found himself excluded from the laboratory of cerebral anatomy, and so without anywhere to deliver his lectures. From then on, he withdrew from academic life and even ceased to attend learned societies.

In 1895 Freud and Breuer published their book *Studies on Hysteria*. Freud maintained that the contents were mainly the product of Breuer's mind, but that the theory put forward was at least partly his responsibility. As well as chapters on the hypnoid state and psychotherapy, this important book contains references to *repression* – the name which Freud gave to the type of forgetting that takes place when the subject matter is so painful that a patient has, as it were, to keep it locked away in his unconscious. The book describes in detail severe cases of hysteria treated by doctors using both hypnosis and what they called the cathartic method. Catharsis takes place within a patient when his emotions concerning some person or some situation are relieved and redeployed. Instead of the feelings being damned up and finding substitute or distorted methods of outlet, they are able to take the original course which was for some reason forbidden to them the first time.

The relationship between Freud and Breuer became difficult when, comparing their observations about the reaction of patients, Freud came to see that it was not just any kind of emotional excitation which lay behind the phenomena of neurosis, but that, inevitably, sexual conflicts or the effect of earlier sexual experiences were present. Freud points out that he could have become aware of the importance of sex far sooner had he taken more seriously chance remarks which Chrobak, the eminent Viennese gynaecologist, Breuer himself and Charcot had made to him earlier. 'Indeed, they told me more than they knew themselves or were prepared to defend', he wrote. 'Nor was I then aware that in deriving hysteria from sexuality I was going back to the very beginnings of medicine and following up a thought of Plato's.'

The frequent coincidence of what was called neurasthenia with disturbances of the sexual function caused Freud to look more closely into the jumble of clinical pictures which his numerous patients presented. He classified these people with anxiety attacks and surrogate symptoms as suffering from *anxiety neurosis*, and limited the term neurasthenia to the rest. Amongst those suffering from anxiety were to be found abnormalities of the sexual life such as *coitus interruptus*, continuous undischarged excitement and sexual abstinence, while neurasthenia seemed to involve inadequate gratification, sometimes accompanied by excessive masturbation and physical debility. Despite the difficulty involved in collecting material from investigations into sexual experience, and in spite of the hostility and disbelief that such theories were bound to receive, Freud felt at ease as a medical man at being able to ascribe to sex, a physical function of supreme biological importance, the causation of mental expressions of what he was now to call the *psychoneuroses*.

In 1892 Freud had begun to question his patients without hypnosis, directing their thoughts and memories towards the origin of their illnesses. He did this having remembered Bernheim's remark that things experienced under hypnosis were only apparently forgotten, and could be brought back into conscious recollection if the physician insisted forcibly enough that the patient could remember them. Freud's guess was that this would be just as true for the forgotten memories of hysterical patients. Each was asked to lie down with closed eyes: sometimes, when no memories seemed available to throw light on the symptom under consideration, Freud would press the patient's forehead with his hand, assuring him or her that some thought or memory would quite certainly come. He would also give his patient strict injunctions to ignore all censorship, telling him to attempt to express every thought, even if he considered it irrelevant, impolite or unpleasant.

He continued urging, pressing and questioning, until one day a patient reproved him for interrupting her flow of thought. Freud took the hint, and by degrees the recommendation for *free association* – i.e. that the patient should say whatever comes into his head, followed by whatever association next presents itself – became the successor to hypnosis. It became then, and remains today, the first and basic procedure for all psychoanalytic treatment.

Freud himself, looking back on *Studies on Hysteria*, regarded the theory attempted there as very incomplete. He wrote, 'We hardly touched on the problem of aetiology [history of the illness], upon the question of the ground in which the pathogenic process takes root'. Recollecting his considerable surprise at realizing that with every case of neurosis some sexual difficulty was present or had been experienced, Freud wrote, 'I took a momentous step. I went beyond the domain of hysteria and began to investigate the sexual life of the so-called neurasthenics who used to visit me in numbers during my consultation hours. This experiment cost me, it is true, my popularity as a doctor, but it brought me convictions which today, thirty years later, have lost none of their force. There was a great deal of equivocation and mystery making to be overcome, but once that had been done it turned out that in all of these patients abuses of the sexual function were present.'

The term *psychoanalysis* was first employed in a paper published in French in March 1896. Freud's discovery and use of free association came, as we have seen, through the necessity of allowing patients the sanction to be completely relaxed and to wander through their thoughts and memories, following only the chain of associations which, Freud discovered, eventually brought them to some point relevant to their difficulties or symptoms. This was a decided change from his earlier hypnotic commands and the urging and pressing to concentrate, which was only marginally related to the cathartic method. Others might have

36

dismissed the early wandering associations which came about once he had ceased to direct his patients' thoughts; but imbued with the principles of causality and determinism, so pronounced in the school of thought inspired by Helmholtz,[1] Freud felt intuitively *that there must be some definite agency, even if not evident, guiding and determining the course of the thinking.* It is more than possible that he followed this intuition because when he was very young he had read an essay written in 1823 by Ludwig Börne. This essay, called *The Art of Becoming an Original Writer in Three Days*, concludes with the practical prescription: 'Take a few sheets of paper, and for three days in succession write down without falsification or hypocrisy everything that comes to mind – what you think of yourself, of your women, of the Turkish war, of Goethe, of the recent criminal case, of the Last Judgement, of those senior to you – when the three days are over you will be amazed at what novel and startling thoughts have welled up in you – that is the art of becoming an original writer in three days.'

Börne had been one of Freud's favourite authors – the first, in fact, in whom he had been absorbed. He had been given his collected works when he was fourteen years old, and they were the only books he had preserved from his adolescent years. Thus Börne's recommendations, made seventy-three years previously, contributed to the *almost* accidental and brilliant arrival of the method of free association, used now by psychoanalysts throughout the world.

Freud soon observed that patients' memories did not stop at the starting point of the symptoms, or even at the unpleasant 'traumatic event' which had previously appeared to be its cause, but instead insisted on going back in a continuous series into childhood itself. This brought him to the realization that the earliest experiences *can constitute a predisposition to neurosis.* He began to see that a traumatic event unmistakably concerned in the genesis of a symptom, although seemingly banal in itself, *only*

[1] During the mid-nineteenth century Hermann Helmholtz's famous school of Medicine revolutionized the thinking of German physiologists and medical teachers, and indeed of scientists all over the world.

produced neurotic effects if it had become associated with some rather similar earlier mental experience or attitude which by itself was not necessarily either traumatic or pathogenic. This manner of reacting to a later event, according to the early associations and experience, he termed *regression,* and it was clear to him that this discovery was noteworthy. It follows automatically that free association led to remembering dreams.

In the summer of 1894 the cooperation with Breuer came to an end. Breuer could not feel nearly as convinced as Freud that disturbances in the sexual life were essential factors in the aetiology of neuroses, and, lacking Freud's self-confidence and powers of resistance, he found the criticisms of his colleagues hard to bear. In fairness to Breuer we should realize that he went a very long way with Freud in *Studies on Hysteria,* stating that, 'The sexual instinct is certainly the most powerful source of lasting increases in excitation and, as such, of the neuroses', that 'conflict between incompatible ideas has a pathogenic effect and is a matter of daily observation. It is mostly a matter of ideas and processes belonging to the sexual life,' and that, 'The greater number and most important of the repressed ideas that lead to hysterical conversion have sexual content.'

One evening, however, after Freud had thanked him for upholding him and agreeing with his views on sexual aetiology at a meeting of the College of Physicians, Breuer turned away saying, 'I don't believe a word of it'. Their relationship cooled until there was virtually nothing left of twenty years of cooperation, friendship and mutual interest.

In thinking about this ruined friendship, four factors must be borne in mind: Freud's confessed need for periodic experiences of intense love and intense hate; the fact that, at the period when he and Breuer began to find each other difficult, Freud was writing his most ardent letters to another friend, Wilhelm Fliess; that between Freud and Breuer lay the inevitable awkwardness caused by the money which Breuer had on various occasions lent Freud; and – perhaps most significant of all – the fact that it was in just these years, the middle nineties, that Freud was in his most revolutionary stage. With the emotional security which his marriage and family gave him, he was far freer intellectually than ever before. His mind was filled with the philosophical problems raised by his daily contact with people seeking treatment for illnesses which appeared to have no organic cause. For a scientist the idea of holding psychological theories not based on physiological data is now, and was for Freud in those days, tremendously questionable. Already in his study, *On Aphasia* he had had to discard the concept that specific thoughts belonged, as it were, to specific brain cells; now, it seemed, he would have to ascribe to unguessed intimate thoughts and feelings, powers over each individual which could radically affect that person's whole life as well as his body. For Freud the doctor it was reassuring to bear in mind that sex is a bodily function, that sexual desire, giving rise to sexual thoughts, is followed by bodily responses and accounts for recognizable physical behaviour; but, confronted with neuroses such as phobias or obsessions, Freud had to steel himself to translate his theory, arrived at through the study of physical symptoms, into a language which could furnish explanation for purely mental disorder.

If one feels compelled to take a step which to the logical, cautious part of one's mind appears risky, one usually takes such a step with a jump. In doing this there is an understandable need to dissociate oneself from anybody who seems to reflect the logical and cautious part of oneself. Hence Freud's rejection of Breuer. He had to venture a jump which he felt Breuer might prevent him from taking.

4 Self-analysis
The Interpretation of Dreams

Had Freud's self-analysis begun earlier, he might perhaps have been softened by the time the disagreement with Breuer became acute, but he only started it in earnest in July 1897. In the previous October his father had died. Freud wrote, 'I had treasured him highly. With his peculiar mixture of deep wisdom and fantastic lightness, he has meant very much in my life. He had passed his time when he died, but inside me the occasion of his death had reawakened all my early feelings. *Now I feel quite uprooted.*' This, then, according to Freud, led him to write *The Interpretation of Dreams*; and the writing of this work went hand in hand with the first year or two of his self-analysis. Here, in the very fabric of Freud's life, can be seen the epitome of the work of psychoanalysis: namely, that if one is fully to understand a human being, his dreams and his free associations are essential.

Through the study of his own dreams, Freud's ability to understand those of his patients increased considerably. For instance, he was fortunate enough to remember a dream about his father which matched with his unconscious fantasies incriminating his father in seduction scenes. He had only begun to realize very slowly that the stories he had heard *and believed* from so many of his patients about the seductions and perverted sexual overtures made by parents were nothing but wishful fantasies. These fantasies are the outcome of the frustrating situation of being a child: part of their function is compensatory. Freud had begun to realize by 1889 that, though very young children are not physically equipped, either chemically or anatomically, to make love to their parents, they do have emotional feelings appropriate to sexual desire.

Through his own analysis, his free associative thoughts and the memories set going by remembering his dreams, which were in turn made comprehensible by studying the formation and work of the dreaming mind, Freud continued to sort out his theory of infantile sexuality. Even as late as 1896 he had gone no further than to write, 'The age of childhood may not be without delicate sexual excitations'. But by October 1897 he realized, through the analytical work on himself, that his father was innocent, and that he had projected on to him all sorts of ideas of his own. Memories came back to him of sexual wishes about his mother (on that occasion of seeing her naked), and of childhood jealousies and quarrels. Memories were recovered about his old nurse, to whom he attributed many of his neurotic troubles – for instance, he recalled that she had once washed him in reddened water in which she had herself previously washed.

Since he was able to ask his mother about his early childhood, he could gain objective confirmation about the truth of his self-analytic findings. The discovery in himself of a past but passionate love for his mother, and jealousy and envy of his father, made him watch for this characteristic in the consulting room, and led him to the famous theory of the *Oedipus complex*. Freud began to think that the Greek legend and the riddle of the sphinx formed a starting point from which one could begin to understand human personality, ambition and satisfaction.

The riddle of the sphinx runs 'What goes on four legs in the morning, two legs at noon and three legs in the twilight?' Oedipus guessed the riddle correctly. The answer was: 'Man – who crawls in infancy, walks upright when in the prime of life and takes a stick to help him when aged'. Freud saw the riddle of the sphinx as the individual's question and answer to himself, the problem of experiencing immaturity, maturity and senility being couched in sexual terms: impotent at first, then potent, and at the end less potent. Because the child contains the two future states while he is still immature, he has within himself desire and fear – the seeds of conflict.

By overcoming his resistance to a belief in the evidence supplied by his dreams, fantasies and recovered memories, Freud achieved two things – a much clearer insight into the resistances of his patients, and a gradual relief from the neurotic anxiety and depressive symptoms which had often plagued him during previous years. Even during his worst suffering he never ceased to carry on with his day-by-day life, continuing with his work, making scientific investigations and caring for and loving his wife and children. Nevertheless, he described his own condition as definitely neurotic.

He knew full well the anguish that comes from a dread of dying, and he often experienced anxiety about travelling by rail. Alterations in his mood between elation and self-confidence on the one hand, and depression, doubt and inhibition on the other often came between him and his writing, and prevented him from concentrating properly on anything but his professional, clinical work. He spent his few leisure hours in a state of restless paralysis, extremely bored, cutting the pages of unread books, looking at maps of ancient Pompeii, unable to continue at anything for long. Sometimes he felt his consciousness so narrowed that he lived almost in a twilight state.

In the lives of most great men there are periods of loneliness and pain which seem almost inseparable from, almost essential to, a period of creativity. Freud's most inspired and original thinking can really be dated as taking place in the last four or five years of the nineteenth century. This followed the great relief from his neurotic condition; indeed, his successive discoveries and the working out of his theories hinged entirely upon his having suffered so much psychological anxiety, depression and sense of disintegration.

It was to his friend Fliess, an ear, nose and throat specialist in Berlin, that Freud mainly confided his doubts and difficulties at this time. If someone complains almost exclusively to one particular person, it often means that unconsciously the sufferer is ascribing his troubles to that person. It seems reasonable to argue that, in so far as Fliess and Freud afforded each other a high degree of mutual admiration, and the theories of each stimulated and reassured the other, a sublimated edition of the parent–child relationship of feeding and caring for each other was in action. Freud was a stoically brave, uncomplaining person, but at this period of his life he revealed to Fliess many of his most intimate feelings, and the state of

42

wretchedness to which he was so often a victim. He wrote to him only once a month, but still there are 152 of these letters. For fifteen years their monthly correspondence flourished. After the death of her husband Frau Fliess sold Freud's letters, but they were recovered after the Second World War, through the perspicacity, courage and cleverness of Freud's illustrious patient and student, Princess Marie Bonaparte. Fliess had many theories which would now be called pseudo-scientific, but which may yet prove to have something in them. He was, for instance, fascinated by numbers, and concocted a theory about periodicity in all vital activities. He laid great stress on the bisexuality of human beings, and on the interrelation between the nose and the nasal cavity and the genitals.

Without the encouragement that Fliess gave, Freud might well not have been so persistent in his search for the inner meaning of the neuroses, and might have taken longer to elucidate unconscious mechanisms. Freud apparently did not wish to involve his family in any part of his search for truth, preferring to keep them out of those conflicts set up by his work. As we saw earlier, Martha fitted in with such a role, and was unwilling to be drawn into scientific or philosophical discussions.

The very fact that Fliess did not meet Freud often, and practised in a different country and with a different type of patient, undoubtedly contributed to the great interest and attraction which each had for the other. Despite Fliess's weakness for numbers, which led him into gross exaggerations, inaccuracies and fantasies about the connexions between biological phenomena and astronomical movements, he acted as a sort of *agent provocateur* to Freud's thinking. It was mainly through his sympathy and his partial understanding that he exerted such an influence on Freud. Jones observed that to all intents and purposes it made Freud dependent on Fliess's opinion in an almost adolescent way. The published letters do not show this. Nowadays we should probably explain many facets of their relationship in terms of projective identification, i.e., that Freud saw in Fliess qualities which he himself needed, yet could not recognize in himself. Through him Freud found permission to 'think new things before being in a position to demonstrate them'. He referred to Fliess as his 'sole public', and said that his encouragement was 'nectar and ambrosia'. His hopes that Fliess's calcutions might solve for good and all the problem of contraception, and his respect for Fliess's knowledge of physics, were distinctly unreal.

It was Fliess to whom Freud wrote that his 'dream child', his great book *The Interpretation of Dreams*, was a 'respectable flop', that his valued relationship with Breuer was at an end, that the theories which he and Fliess held were 'far ahead of our time', and that they should expect, 'no recognition in our lifetime'.

During his self-analysis it was Fliess to whom he confessed that he had gone through an inner crisis and that Fliess would find him aged. He wrote, 'Your presence would have been invaluable to me during the catastrophic collapse'. He wrote, too, that although he was, 'Inwardly deeply impoverished, I have just plucked up enough courage to start rebuilding castles in the air'. He wrote this in March 1900, and it is probable that we shall never know quite what he meant when he wrote in the same letter, 'I conquered my depression with the aid of a special intellectual diet, and now under the influence of the distraction it is slowly healing'. At the same time he refused an invitation to meet Fliess again, saying, 'In your company I should inevitably attempt to grasp everything consciously and tell you all about it; we should talk rationally and scientifically, and the upshot would be that I should unburden my woes to you for five whole days and come back agitated and dissatisfied for the summer. No one can help me in what oppresses me, it is my cross which I must bear and, heaven knows, my back is getting noticeably bent under it.' With these words Freud illustrates the turmoil and sense of loneliness which every analysand can recognize. He was unique in learning about this without the help of the trained concern which every analyst has for his patient. When Freud produced his free associations, or thought of his dreams, there was no impartial recipient to hear them and sort them according to a well-defined theory, no listening person on to whom to project the current feelings of love and trust, hate and distrust.

44

In another letter to Fliess, Freud says of a patient, R. that, 'The analysis of a subsequent case similar to R. would not take so long'. This illustrates Freud's lack of awareness in those days of the individuality of each analytic case. As a physical doctor he thought then that knowledge of the aetiology and gravity of one set of psychological symptoms, and experience of a previous treatment, would enable him to shorten other treatments, just as proper diagnoses enable medical men to give shorter and more effective treatments to well-known bodily illness. Nowadays we know that this is not true of neurosis and analytic patients. But Freud did realize how hard it was to treat himself, and in his self-analysis he became very aware of the degree and depth of resistance to treatment. He witnessed his own unwillingness to accept analytic interpretations and insights into primitive unconscious loves and hates.

Through the process of dreaming, free associating and recovering childhood memories, through his realization of the influence of the past upon the thoughts and feelings, ambitions and fears of the present, Freud slowly cleared away for himself much of the irrational anxiety and moodiness and many of the mental blocks which had prevented him from seeing through the inhibitions and problems of his patients. Reciprocally, too, he was able to make use of his experience with his patients to uncover and explore areas of his own personality. Through his work on himself, Freud not only began to understand what had made the predisposition to neurosis in his patients; he also started to trace the characteristics essential in any psychotherapist who hopes to cure or ameliorate the condition of those suffering from a neurosis. First, he recognized that a psychotherapist must have the ability to keep still, and also be totally permissive towards all forms of thought and fantasy however irrelevant or shocking. Secondly, he must be able to develop a hovering attention (neither too absent-minded nor yet too concentrated), and a clarity of vision and purpose which enable him to remain sympathetic, yet sufficiently detached and objective to see through the patient's symptoms, chatter and dreams to the inner and upside-down meaning which lies behind.

45

Without his introspection as to what kind of mental reception he, Freud, gave as a therapist to the material which he, Freud, produced as a patient, we should never have learned the technique employed by psychoanalysts; nor should we have learned that in order to treat neurotics psychotherapists must first have the experience of being a patient and of being listened to by an experienced analyst for at least a couple of years. Nowadays this training lasts for four years or more.

In his letters to Fliess Freud described some of his patients, and included drafts concerning his theories about infantile sexuality, the aetiology of hysteria and neuroses, how anxiety originates, melancholia, paranoia, migraine and the neurosis of defence. From this alone can be seen what an important mental clearing-house the friendship and the letters were. No wonder that the person who could receive and respond to these ideas, was of such inestimable value, for Freud was beginning to accept as inevitable the fact that his theories were, in his own words 'odious' and 'bound to put people off'. Fliess was full of novel ideas, but he was much less sensible about people's rejection of them. His touchiness about Freud's apparent neglect of his views on periodic laws and left-handedness required all Freud's small store of tact to smooth things over.

Their last meeting, at Achensee in 1900, saw a head-on clash, the details of which are unclear. What seems to have happened is that Fliess replied to some criticism of Freud's about the periodic laws by calling him 'only a thought reader', and by the accusation that 'he read his own thoughts into his patients'. Moreover, although it was Fliess who early in their friendship had raised the whole question of bisexuality, Freud seemed to have forgotten this, and appeared to believe that other influences, as well as Fliess's, had led him to work in this field. For two more years Freud tried to save the personal part of the friendship, though he recognized that 'the old scientific intercourse could never be resumed'.

In subsequent writings Freud mentions Fliess a number of times. He states that it was from him that he adopted the terms *latency period* (the years between the ages of five or six to eleven or twelve, after the influence of the Oedipus complex has abated, till puberty), and *sublimation* (the unconscious transferring of primitive instinctive drives of aggression and sex into civilized efforts to serve and create). Much later he showed great understanding of his feelings for Fliess when he wrote of himself to Ferenczi, 'A part of the homosexual cathexis has been withdrawn and made use of to enlarge my own ego'.

As with many other discoveries, it could be said that Freud was really looking for one thing when he found another. Being supremely open-minded he did not brush aside this other, but allowed himself to be led off on what could have been a wild goose chase. In actual fact this led him to what he called the royal road to the unconscious – namely, the study and interpretation of dreams. Listening to the free associations of his patients, and then to his own at the beginning of his long self-analysis, he realized how often thoughts, when they were allowed to run freely, would meet with the memory of a dream; and from these he began to glimpse the language proper of the unconscious. Freud himself was a good dreamer. In those days, when he studied and began to understand the contents of dreams, it was not known, as it is now, that dreaming is essential to mental life. Nor was it known then that everyone dreams, but that by no means everyone can retain the memory of dreams on waking or recapture them later on. But Freud was aware of Hughlings Jackson's pronouncement, 'Find out about dreams, and you will find out about insanity'. Some years earlier, in a *Project for a Scientific Psychology* which Freud had sent to Fliess after the two friends had met in Berlin, he had written, 'Dreams contain the psychology of the neurosis in a nutshell'. As he took more and more notice of dreams he was able to form a theory about the way they function and the reasons for their appearance. In *The Interpretation of Dreams*, which he always felt was by far his most original work, he put forward a completely new view of dreaming.

It took him two years to write the book, which was published in 1900. It was hardly reviewed or remarked on at all when it first appeared in an edition of only 600 copies. This appears not to have surprised Freud in any

His complete understanding of the resistance in the
:ious mind to study or acceptance of the dynamics
content of the unconscious meant that he did not
)lain of his lack of popular success or even expect any.
d not depress him to think that he 'would only be
ght of as an early pioneer when some later investigator
es the same discoveries'; what mattered to him was the
fact that he had reached his goal – namely, the achievement
of solving for himself problems of human personality and
mental life about which he was so unceasingly curious.

The book begins by alluding to the varied literature then
available on dreams, and refers to the respect and awe
which they commanded in classical antiquity, among
primitive peoples and in religious organizations. Freud
agreed with earlier psychologists and philosophers that the
dream was both remote from the material of everyday
waking life and yet always employing elements from part
of the experiences or thoughts from the previous day or
week. He also believed that dreams provide evidence that
we store memories of events long past – even events
happening during the second and third year of life. He
discovered this through a dream which he had had when he
was about forty, about someone who seemed to be a doctor
in Freiberg, but whose features reminded him of one of his
schoolmasters. On questioning his mother, it emerged
that these two men had each lost an eye. It was thirty-
eight years since Freud had seen this doctor! Thus he
found with ever-increasing accuracy that the dreams he
met with demonstrated that 'Nothing which we have once
psychically possessed is ever entirely lost'. This finding,
of course, reinforced his belief in the comprehension
within the unconscious of all experiences, from the day of
birth onwards. Hypnosis had previously demonstrated this
in people who went into deep trances. Freud listed some
of the external stimuli which evoke in a sleeping person
dreams that make meaningful the sensations which the
stimuli set going. For example, one common response to
the bell of any alarm clock is to dream of some stream of
sound. One man, on different occasions, had three such
dreams in response to his alarm clock, the first of church
bells, the second of sleigh bells and the third of breaking

in the unconscious mind and are only allowed into consciousness after having passed through a form of inspection, a restriction and distortion of their original strength. This inspection process Freud called the censor. He showed that this censor so alters the appearance of the original wish or drive that the content of the dream – the story, as it were – seems to the dreamer on waking to be either untrue, meaningless, ludicrous or stupid. Thus the truly significant basis of the dream is changed into a more or less insignificant or nonsensical kind of memory which could not logically attract serious consideration.

Freud gave very many examples of dreams to show the different kinds of dream-work employed to keep unconscious desires and fears secret, and to conceal the egocentricity of primitive thinking. He recognized dream-work as demonstrating what he called:

1. Condensation (this includes puns, nonsense words, collective figures and numbers);
2. Displacement; distortion; reversal;
3. Elaboration.

For instance, a girl dreamed that she saw her sister's only surviving child lying dead in the very same place where only a few years earlier she had actually seen the dead body of her sister's other child. During the dream she felt no pain over this, but on waking naturally felt that the dream could not possibly represent any wish of hers. However, it came to light that it had been beside the dead child's coffin that she had first seen and spoken to the man with whom she was still in love. The *condensation* in the dream therefore took her both forwards and backwards, for, argued the dream-work, if another child died she would be back in the same situation – i.e. meeting the man she loved. She was longing for such a meeting but had tried to fight against the longing, although on the day preceding the dream she had bought a ticket for a lecture which he was giving. Her dream was what Freud calls, 'A simple dream of impatience such as one experiences before journeys, visits to a theatre, or other pleasures. The dream was somehow anticipating her actual enjoyment.' But to conceal the longing the situation was *displaced* and *reversed* to the sort of event which contained the very opposite of pleasure.

Freud describes this interaction between unconscious and conscious as though, 'One person who was dependent upon a second person had to make a remark which was bound to be disagreeable to the ears of the second', and, 'On the basis of this simile we have arrived at the concepts of dream distortion and censorship'. He continued, 'It is the second person, however, who controls access to consciousness, and thus can ban the first person from such access'.

Writing about the anxiety of examination dreams, Freud agreed with a colleague who had pointed out that this sort of dream only occurred to persons who had passed the examination in question: it never occurred to those who had failed. Analysts have found that the latent content of such dreams usually concerns the anxious anticipation of a future responsible task where there could once more be a chance of disgrace of failure. Thus the wish for success is fulfilled at the end of the process, during the waking moments when the dreamer realizes that he has in reality safely surmounted a feared situation. The same interpretation holds good for dreams where the dreamer forgets the lines he has to speak in a play or on a public occasion.

Freud alluded to the lightning speed of the dream process when he described the dream of a man, who, when he was ill in bed, dreamed of the Reign of Terror during the French Revolution. He was summoned before the Tribunal, saw Robespierre, Marat and the other leaders and was asked to give an account of himself. He was sentenced to death and accompanied by a crowd to the scaffold. The executioner tied him to the plank, it tipped, and the knife fell. He felt his head severed from his trunk and woke in fearful anxiety, only to find that the headboard of his bed had fallen! It had actually struck the cervical vertebrae just where a guillotine knife would fall. The dream-work had been crowded into the space of time elapsing between the sleeper's perception of the knock from the fallen headboard and the moment of his proper awakening.

During the awakening, *the censorship which pertains to consciousness* recovers its strength, much of which has been disarmed by sleep. It can, therefore, wipe out all the dream messages that entered the conscious from the unconscious, either by simply forgetting them – which most of us do – or by regarding them as absurd and useless. It often happens that in the narrating of a dream an incident is suddenly remembered which had originally been forgotten. The forgetting of this incident is certainly in itself of real significance, just because of the need of the conscious mind to disregard that particular item of the dream: no doubt that item carried a message of great importance to the unconscious life, one which the censor could not at first allow to penetrate into conscious memory.

Freud's theory that dreams, like the symptoms of hysterical or obsessional patients, spell out processes and drives from the unconscious which would not be considered respectable by the conscious mind, gained him no immediate respect, friends, or wealth. He was asked again and again, 'Why must we suspect the human psyche of such duality, egocentricity, eroticism?' Before the first world war most people in western society believed implicitly and ardently in the firm establishment of civilization and regarded mankind as completely mature. Of course they knew that regrettable instances of 'wickedness' were still to be observed, but it was thought that all 'wickedness' would fade away on encountering the benevolent forces of Christian education and scientific investigation. The growing belief in psychoanalysis, both as a therapeutic procedure and as a mode of understanding human beings, was due in no small way to the world-wide experience of bloodshed and hatred. People were no longer able to deny their own primitive reactions to primitive situations, and at last found it necessary to credit human psychology with a double life – the civilized and the primitive. Conscience was seen to be much more of an unconscious process than previous moralists and preachers had realized.

By the late 1920s many intelligent and thoughtful people had read Freud. Several hundred had experienced analysis. They read *The Interpretation of Dreams, Three Essays on the Theory of Sexuality* and *The Psychopathology of Everyday Life*. These can still be pondered over and read by all those who want to understand or be of help to their fellow creatures.

5 *The Psychopathology of Everyday Life*

Signorelli	**B**otticelli	**B**oltraffio
Herzegovina	**Bo**snia	Trafoi

Herr Sir, what can I say,....(Repressed thoughts of Death and Sexuality)

Freud began to write *The Psychopathology of Everyday Life* in 1900, though it was not published till 1904. It concerns the same type of phenomena as dreams, but observes errors and slips made during waking hours. The model above is his illustration of how he came to forget the name of Signorelli, the painter responsible for the famous frescoes of the Last Judgement in the cathedral at Orvieto. He was sharing a carriage with a stranger going south from Dubrovnik, and had been discussing travelling in Italy. Freud substituted two names in his efforts to remind himself of the correct name – first Botticelli and then Boltraffio.

In trying to elucidate why he should have forgotten Signorelli, Freud knew at once that he must freely associate, and that this process would eventually lead him to find out the reasons for his repression. As a result of his work with dream interpretation, he began by looking for displacement. He realized that before the discussion about travel in Italy they had talked of the customs of the Turks who had lived in Bosnia and Herzegovina. Freud had related that these people always showed full confidence in their physician, and offered complete submission to fate. If relatives happened to hear that there was no help for their patient they would answer, 'Sir [*Herr* in German] what can I say? I know if he could be saved you would save him.' It was in these sentences that the partially

54

punning words Bosnia, Herzegovina and Herr were to be found which could be inserted as a free association series between Signorelli and Botticelli and Boltraffio. (See diagram at the beginning of this chapter.)

Freud realized that, while he had related this anecdote, he was conscious of not referring to the way Turks value sexual pleasure. He had thought how strange was their misery and despair at any sexual disturbance, compared to their resignation at the prospect of loss of life. One Turk had actually said to a colleague of his, 'You know, sir [Herr], if that [meaning sex] ceases, life no longer has any charm'. This unrelated part of the story, this virtual prohibition, must, Freud realized, have had as its unconscious association another piece of information, this time concerning one of his patients. It was while he was staying at Trafoi that this patient had taken his own life because of a sexual disturbance for which Freud had been trying to treat him for some time. Thus the theme of death and sexuality was activated in Freud's unconscious, despite his conscious and intentional deviation from it. The disagreeableness of the theme and his distress at the patient's death set up in him a 'need to forget'. This need missed its aim, however, for, while he was really wanting to forget his grief and the puzzling problems involved in death and sexuality, he only managed to forget something unimportant to him, the name Signorelli.

The Psychopathology of Everyday Life abounds with illustrations of mistakes and lapses of memory such as this: mistakes in speech, in reading and writing; the forgetting of foreign words, of impressions and resolutions and of wrongly carried out or symptomatic and chance actions. There is also a chapter about superstition. Wherever possible Freud took notice of errors, and if it was at all seemly he got the person who had made them to account for them. When a patient makes errors during an analysis, they can be of real value; they help to elucidate personal problems, and the unconscious reasons for some of the patient's likes and dislikes. For example, a teacher forgot and misquoted Keats's *Ode to Apollo*, enabling Freud to uncover the pain she was concealing, even from herself, caused by a very unhappy love affair she had had long ago.

55

As in the interpretation of his own dreams, Freud preferred to use examples from his own life and the experiences of his acquaintances, since he was always mindful that, if he quoted his patients' material, his critics would point to this as evidence that his theories could only be tenable with regard to sick people. He himself felt absolutely sure that the mechanisms which were so pronounced among neurotics were also present, though in less troublesome ways, among the healthy. He wrote that all seemingly innocent and casual errors, like slips of the tongue, were the outcome of some personal complex at work in the deep unconscious of the person who made the slip. He maintained that the slip was indicative of some intimate subject matter which might afford pain either to the person who made the mistake or to those around him. The slip, therefore, was in some way associated with unconscious material, though it was conscious material – the speech or activity – which became distorted. The only physiological explanation of such errors with which Freud agreed was that when people are tired, ill, drunk or under some provocation, they become increasingly accident prone; he himself would often forget names at the onset of one of his migraines.

Freud held that areas where such accidents might happen, either insignificant accidents like reversing words or substituting a word with the opposite meaning, or more serious distortions, have always something to do with personal difficulties known about but censored within the person under stress. He believed, for example, that although a circulatory or functional disorder within the brain could and might distort a person's speech and actions, yet the nature of the distortion would still have to do with some unconscious self-reference, either personal, familial or professional. Thus the emotions of wishful thinking, love, hate, guilt, shame, and the need to conceal would all be found to be behind many sorts of seemingly chance mistakes, just as they can be traced in the interpretation of a dream. Likewise, the same processes of repression, inhibition, displacement, condensation and concealment can be expected to be at work beneath a mistake, just as they are beneath a dream. Meringer and Mayer, physiologists who concerned themselves with some aspects of human behaviour, had written about mistakes in speech and about forgetting words, but Freud found most of their explanations superficial; he thought they showed little understanding of basic human psychology. All the same, he agreed with much of what Wundt, the famous German psychologist, had published earlier, especially the theory that the uninhibited stream of sound and word associations produced by speech, and the actual relaxation needed to produce them, allowed for the entry of psychic influences. Freud stated that he had never found an example of a mistake in speech which he could attribute solely to what Wundt had called the 'contact effect of sound': he maintained that invariably he would discover some startling influence outside the intended form of words. One example of this is the mistake made by the Austrian President at the Opening of Parliament, who ended his address by saying, 'And now I have pleasure in declaring the session closed'. Here Wundt's idea of the contact of sound is relevant, since it is likely that the President had used this flow of words before to declare a session closed, and had therefore fallen into a habit of speech, but apparently he was also pessimistic about the coming session, and so would have liked it to be at an end. Thus the wish escaped his internal censorship, and caused this famous slip of the tongue. Such mistakes are now known throughout the world as 'Freudian slips'.

Freud illustrates his own egoism – a trait which he helped so many others to notice in themselves – by quoting various mistakes which he made in reading. Once he misread a letter concerning the serious illness of a friend, attributing the grave condition to the wife rather than to the husband. He did this because the man was associated in his mind with another and dearer friend who had the same disease and about whom Freud felt anxious; in the latter case, therefore, he wished the wife to be the sufferer. He also relates how he seemed always to read on shopsigns the word 'Antiquities', for he was an avid collector.

Freud does not spare himself when he analyses his own blunders in writing the wrong date on a letter or the wrong sum on a cheque. He goes into the associations connected with these errors, seeing eventually that although consciously he could not believe that he still feared poverty, or regretted a generous action, these emotions were in fact present in his unconscious. He points to printers' errors in newspapers, in the London Bible of 1631 (where the negative was left out of the seventh commandment!) and in the German Bible of 1580, where the word Narr (which means fool) was printed instead of Herr (man) in God's instruction to Eve that Adam shall be her man and rule over her! Errors such as writing 'owing to foreseen circumstances' instead of 'unforeseen', and addressing envelopes wrongly because of wishes or resentment, are described in order to demonstrate how primitive reactions find ways of emerging, despite the considerate and polite manner with which a civilized person hopes to keep himself in control. Freud stresses something which earlier observers had noted: that few people accept such slips calmly, and whenever possible they dispute the fact that they have made an error. This, he says, only emphasizes how important to the unconscious such a 'give away' is.

During his schooldays Freud could reproduce from memory whole pages of textbooks; to some extent this capacity remained with him until the end of his medical studies. Since then he had steadily lost control over his memory, but had recently come to use an artifice to enable him to recall far more than he could have done otherwise. If, for instance, a patient told him that he had consulted him before and Freud was totally unable to remember anything about it, he helped himself by guessing – that is, he allowed a number of years to come to his mind quickly, running backwards from the present time. He would generally find that a guess came up from the unconscious; and whenever these memories could be checked by records or definite information from the patient, he was seldom found to be more than six months out; and it often happened that in the course of the consultation other details of the previous first visit returned to him. Freud went on to say that the same thing would happen, 'When I meet an acquaintance, and from politeness inquire after his small child. When the father tells of its progress, I try to fancy how old the child now is. I control my estimate by the information given, and at most I make a mistake of a month, in older children three months. I cannot state, however, what basis I have for my estimate, but of late I have grown so bold that I offer my estimate spontaneously, and still run no risk of grieving the father by displaying ignorance in regard to his offspring. *Thus I extend my conscious memory by invoking my larger unconscious memory.*'

Many followers of Freud have done the same thing either by remembering this passage in his book or by stumbling upon this faculty independently. What Freud neglected to point out was that he himself – like many doctors, social workers, journalists, and novelists – had a great need to feel informed about the people he was in contact with. This need constitutes an almost personal interest that can overcome many of the blocks and barriers which would maintain ordinary forgetfulness in less involved listeners.

Freud knew that he did not belong to the category of people who are generally forgetful or distracted. From his observations of such people he conjectured that the motive behind their behaviour was 'an unusually large amount of unavowed disregard for others'. This is a succinct way of expressing a diagnosis almost universally felt and agreed on.

Freud illustrates how the desire for recognition can cause false remembering, the ante-dating of scientific observations, for instance, or a failure to remember that an original idea was first suggested by another person. He called attention to Darwin's 'golden rule for the scientific worker', to make a written note of every published fact, observation or thought which is *contrary* to his own general results, for, Darwin had discovered, these are almost certain to be forgotten or disregarded. He quotes his American follower, Brill, who summed up the complex about the payment of money in the words, 'We are more apt to mislay letters containing bills than cheques', and lays emphasis on the importance of money and possessions in the primitive unconscious.

Likening the 'service of women' to military service (which demands that nothing relating to that service be forgotten), Freud points out that with 'their fine under-

59

standing of unconscious mental processes' women always take more seriously such slips as a failure by a friend or acquaintance to recognize them in the street, for, he said they conclude that if they are held to be of real consequence then they would surely be noticed. Similarly, military authorities accept forgetting as an excuse for not polishing buttons, since admitting disgust at performing this menial task would court far greater punishment.

The unconscious reasons for mixing up keys – taking out the home key to gain entrance to the office, or vice versa – are described vividly both by Freud and by his one-time pupils and colleagues, Ernest Jones and Hanns Sachs. He also explains the reasons for walking up one flight of stairs beyond the proper destination for a customary visit. Twice he did this himself, once because of an ambitious daydream which he had at the time he was going upstairs, and once because of irritation with a criticism of his works which said that, 'He always goes too far'. This, he comments, he must mentally have replaced by the less respectful expression 'climbs too high'. (It seems that he partly agreed with his critic!)

Freud went into great detail to show how an action which is carried out erroneously can be a form of self-reproach. The instance he quotes shows to what lengths he went to demonstrate honestly and carefully his own inner life. A tuning-fork and a small hammer for testing reflexes lay as a rule side by side on his desk. In a hurry to catch a train one day, he took the tuning-fork instead of the hammer. He noticed the mistake because of the extra weight in his pocket. Anyone not keyed up to pay attention to such slips would have blamed the haste of the moment for the error; but Freud asked himself who it was who had last grasped the tuning-fork. It happened that only a few days previously an idiot child whom Freud was testing had been fascinated by it. 'Does it mean,' Freud wondered, 'that I am an idiot?' His next association was to the word – hammer – and then to the Hebrew word *chamer*, which means ass. Furthermore, Freud realized that he was travelling on the railway line he had used on an earlier consultation. On that occasion he had diagnosed the patient in question as a case of hysteria, though the man had actually been suffering from multiple sclerosis. At this new consultation, Freud had to decide whether a patient was hysterical after a fall from a balcony or whether he had a spinal injury. He deduced that his unconscious wanted to caution him against being an 'idiot' this time, thus reminding himself of the delicacy of discriminating between hysterical conditions and symptoms which could be organic.

Freud decided that the following conditions had to be fulfilled before a faulty psychic action can be said to have taken place.

1. It must not exceed behaviour already firmly established as being 'within normal limits'.
2. It must look like a momentary and temporary disturbance, affecting an action which is usually correctly performed.
3. It must be something which, if corrected by others, is easily recognized as having need of correction.
4. If it is the mistaken person who perceives the faultiness of the action, it must seem capable of explanation as having happened through inattention or as being 'purely accidental'.

In the chapter on determinism, Freud goes on to illustrate that a name or a number thought of at random inevitably has some connexion with unconscious material already categorized and retained. He illustrates this with the example of how, when he was searching for an assumed name for a female case history which he wanted to publish, only one came to mind, Dora. When he thought about this, he realized that on the previous evening he had learnt that his sister had a nurse for her children who was called Rosa; but as this was also his sister's name the nurse-maid was known as Dora instead. 'Poor people,' Freud had thought, 'they cannot even retain their own names.' (That the patient in this case history was symbolically a kind of domestic slave to her illness is significant.)

The same thing was true of numbers. Freud wrote to a friend with jocular exaggeration that he had just finished reading the proof sheets of *The Interpretation of Dreams*, and did not intend to make a single further change even if it contained 2467 mistakes! When he tried to explain to himself the choice of that number, he remembered that before writing this letter he had read about a General E.M. who had recently been retired, and whom he had once attended while he was a military medical student. Freud was twenty-four at the time. This gives the number 24 in the figure 2467. By adding to 24 his present age, 43, Freud arrived at the figure 67. He realized then that he was really hoping to be retired with honour in the same number of years as had preceded his first meeting with the general. Freud repeated this testing of arbitrarily chosen numbers many times, never failing to find some predetermined reason for the selection.

Admittedly, however, there is also a predetermined skill or lack of skill in the free associative process. If there is a great deal of *unconscious resistance* to finding out unconscious motives for choices or mistakes, then the first free associations which come to mind will not inevitably lead the seeker to the source – indeed, they may lead him away from it. On the whole Freud was better motivated to explore his unconscious than most of us. Very few people can analyse themselves at all satisfactorily without having had analysis from a qualified analyst or psychotherapist. Freud himself recognized and admitted inadequacies in his own analysis of himself, realizing that he had certain blind spots about his own psyche because he had not been analysed by someone else.

In order to make clear the sources of superstition, Freud refers to the mental illness known as paranoia. This causes some people to feel threatened and suspicious of the innocent or natural behaviour of others around them. These suspicions are sometimes called ideas of reference: the sufferer *projects* out on to others bad intentions which a part of his unconscious mind knows he harbours within himself.

In his chapter on superstition Freud relates an incident when a coachman, who knew perfectly well the address of a very old lady whom Freud had to visit daily, made a mistake and drove him to a house with the same number, but in a different though similar-looking street. Freud wrote that had he been superstitious he might have regarded the coachman's error as an ill-omen foretelling the old lady's death (to arrive at a home where she was not). He went on to state that had he absentmindedly made the mistake himself it would not have been at all fortuitous, but would have pointed to his own expectation that he would not be seeing her much longer. Thus superstitions, Freud maintained, arise when people project their own suspicions, expectations or wishes on to the independent actions of others. What Freud did not go into was the cause which determined the coachman's error; he used this illustration merely to show how superstitious beliefs come about. It is here that Freud makes his conception of chance quite clear by stating, 'I believe in outer (real) chance but not in inner (psychic) accidents. The case is reversed with the superstitious person. He knows nothing of the motives of his chance or faulty actions but believes in the existence of psychic contingencies. So he is inclined to attribute meaning to external chance, and to see in accidents expressions of something hidden but outside himself. Thus the differences between me and a superstitious person are that he projects the motive to the outside while I look for it in myself. Secondly, he explains the accident by an event which I trace to a thought. What he considers hidden corresponds with me to the unconscious, and my compulsion is not to let chance pass as chance but to explain it as common to both of us.'

Freud went on to liken mythology and 'even the most modern religions' to 'psychology projected into the outer world'. He stated that, having regard to life in pre-scientific times, superstition was consistent and justified. (By pre-scientific times Freud was really referring to the long epoch before man recognized the size and nature of his unconscious!) A nice point is made when Freud wrote that the Roman who gave up an important undertaking because he saw a flock of birds of ill-omen was acting in accord with the superstitious beliefs of his day, but that the Roman who refused such an undertaking because he stumbled on his own threshold was a true psychologist, since something in him, by stumbling, showed an appreciation of internal conflict and doubt, the presence of a hidden counter force to his express intention, and that this factor might weaken him, since a person's success depends on the integration of his psychic forces.

Freud concludes this important book with the sentence, 'But the common character of the mildest as well as the severest cases to which faulty and chance actions contribute *lies in the ability to refer the phenomena to unwelcome, repressed psychic material, which though pushed away from consciousness is nevertheless not robbed of all capacity to express itself.*'

In his own short autobiography he wrote about his research into the psychopathology of everyday life, 'Since dreams turned out to be symptoms, and slips and errors to share common features with dreams – namely, the repression of impulses, substitute formations, compromise formations and the dividing of the conscious and unconscious into various psychical systems – then psychoanalysis was no longer a subsidiary science in the field of psychopathology but rather a foundation for a new and deeper science of the mind which would be equally indispensable for the understanding of normal people.'

6 Friends and enemies

Freud kept the manuscripts of *Jokes and Their Relation to the Unconscious* and *Three Essays on the Theory of Sexuality* on two adjoining tables and wrote now on one and now on the other, as the mood took him. They were both ready for publication by 1905. The first contains some of his best writing but is one of his least read books, perhaps because the psychological mechanisms lying behind wit and humour are difficult to apprehend until one has become used to grasping them in simpler situations.

The second brought down on Freud more odium than anything else he wrote. *The Interpretation of Dreams* was held to be fantastic and ridiculous, but *Three Essays* was thought shockingly wicked. Freud's assertions that children are born with sexual urges which undergo a complicated development before reaching the familiar adult form, and that their first sexual objects are their parents, or those who represent their parents, was abominable to contemporary readers. His prediction that his conclusions would eventually be taken for granted was right; but for about twenty years he was the subject of criticism and abuse. In the eyes of the medical profession it was held to be unforgivable when, after four years of hesitation, he decided to publish a case history generally referred to as the 'Dora Analysis'. Intimate details about a young girl who suffered from an obscure hysteria, implying that she had various perverted tendencies, did not seem to his colleagues a proper subject-matter for publication. They refused to see how it could enable students of psychopathology to elucidate and help similar cases.

Yet when one reads Freud's actual works one is amazed at the tentative, considerate terms in which his theories are put forward. He wrote that, in half his cases of severe hysterias and obsessional neuroses, syphilitic parents or grandparents could be traced. The possibility of biological causes for neurotic manifestations was never excluded from his thinking. Thus the accusation that psychoanalysis attributes everything to psychopathology is now, as it was then, very wide of the mark. How wrong this accusation is can be seen if one looks at the end of the summary of *Three Essays*, which runs, 'The unsatisfactory conclusion that emerges from these investigations of the disturbances of sexual life is that we know far too little of the biological processes constituting the essence of sexuality to be able to construct from our fragmentary information a theory adequate to the understanding alike of normal and of pathological conditions.'

During the first three or four years of this century – when, as a result of working daily with neurotic patients, Freud wrote and published the books which laid down the structure of his theories and the lines on which he intended to analyse and teach others to analyse – he was almost entirely on his own. He called these the 'years of splendid isolation', and later described this period as having the advantage of being without competitors and without badly informed opponents. Nor was there any need to read up or collect extensive literature, as he had had to do in his neurological years, for none existed in the field he was opening up. During this time he had to develop and maintain complete independence from the opinions of others.

To get an idea of the opposition to Freud one has to remember that his followers were regarded as sexual perverts, and were thought to be a real threat to the community. At a meeting of German neurologists in 1910 the chairman banged his fist on the table, saying of psychoanalysis, 'This is not a topic for a scientific meeting: it is a matter for the police'. The Medical Society in Budapest agreed that Freud's writing was 'nothing but pornography', and that 'the proper place for psychoanalysts was prison'. In 1908 an Australian, Donald Fraser, who had brought together a small group of people to study Freud's writings, had to relinquish his position as a Presbyterian minister; and that same year Ernest Jones was forced to resign a neurological appointment in London because he had made inquiries into the sex life of his patients. In 1909 Wulff, a disciple in Berlin, was dismissed from the institution where he worked, and Pfister, a Swiss pastor with whom Freud had become friendly, was several times in trouble with his superiors once his adherence to psychoanalysis was known, though he did not have to leave his church. His colleague, Schneider, was, however, dismissed from the headship of a seminary, and the Swedish philologist, Sperber, was ruined by having his *Dozentship* denied to him after he had written an essay on the sexual origin of speech.

Until 1905 Freud and his writing had been quietly ignored or referred to in a short sentence or two, but once he had published the Dora analysis critics took a more active line. Freud was relieved at this, preferring open opposition and abuse to being ignored. One accusation, soon to become familiar, was first made by doctors in Hamburg: 'Freud's methods are dangerous because they simply breed sexual ideas in patients'. Another was, 'Freud's treatment is on a par with the massage of the genital organs', and a third, 'Other populations are not as sensual as that of Vienna'. Even as late as 1916 a Berlin professor published a tirade against Freudian theory, saying, 'In the great times in which we live such old wives' psychiatry is doubly repulsive'. When his notice was drawn to this Freud remarked, 'Now we know what we have to expect from the great times. No matter – an old Jew is tougher than a royal Prussian Teuton.' Nearly all the criticism could be reduced to two pronouncements – namely, that Freud's interpretations were arbitrary and his conclusions, being repulsive, must be untrue.

It never crossed Freud's mind to reply publicly to such diatribes; this seemed to him a pointless waste of time. Although he was exceedingly sensitive he normally responded to criticism only by continuing his work and producing further evidence. He never wanted to coerce his fellows into believing his theories, and he disliked debates and even public scientific discussion, the object of which he soon saw to be mainly controversial, an outlet for personal aggression or spite. However, though he was impervious to most insults, he did object greatly to those people who implied that his experience with patients counted for nothing, and that his ideas were 'sucked out of our fingers or put together at the writing table'. He minded, too, that academic and polite Viennese society ostracized him. His objectivity and good sense about public criticism from his colleagues is best illustrated by a quotation from a letter to Stärcke, a Dutch analyst, who was about to speak at a medical congress in Holland: 'Your idea of persuading society through suggestion has two things against it. In the first place, it contemplates something impossible, and in the second it departs from the prototype of psychoanalytic treatment. *One has really to treat doctors as we do our patients*, therefore not by suggestion but by evoking their resistances and conflict.' And later in the same letter, having referred to those who would stay 'bogged down in their resistances till they reel by the indirect pressure of the growth of public opinion', he goes on, 'To compile statistics as you propose is at present impossible. To begin with, we work with much smaller numbers than other doctors who devote so much less time to individuals. Then the necessary uniformity is lacking which alone can form a basis for any statistics. What do we call a severe case? Moreover, I could not regard my own results in the past twenty years as comparable, since my technique fundamentally changed in that time. And what should we do about the numerous cases which are only partially analysed and those where treatment had to be discontinued for external reasons? The therapeutic point of view, however, is not the only one for which psychoanalysis claims interest, nor is it the most important. So there is a great deal to be said on the subject even without putting therapy in the forefront.'

In relatively recent times the implications of the last sentence scandalized many people other than doctors. To them it is bad enough that Freud and the Freudians should claim that physical methods of treating neurosis are wrong; to state that psychoanalysis has more to offer than simply the amelioration of mental trouble, to believe that it can clarify, or account for, the thoughts and actions of normal people in modern or historical times, outraged all those who prefer man and his behaviour to remain enigmatic.

By degrees more and more abstracts of Freud's writings

were appearing in psychiatric periodicals, as well as lengthy reviews of them, particularly in Anglo-Saxon countries. The beginning of the famous Vienna Psycho-Analytical Society must be dated from the time when Max Kahane and Rudolf Reitler, both doctors, began to attend Freud's university lectures on the psychology of the neuroses (Freud had been made Professor Extraordinarius in 1902). Kahane introduced Wilhelm Stekel, a Viennese physician who had written a paper on coitus in childhood, and it was Stekel's idea that he, Kahane, Reitler, and Alfred Adler, also a Viennese doctor, should meet every Wednesday to discuss Freud's work. They met round the oblong table in Freud's waiting-room, and became known as the 'Psychological Wednesday Society'. They were joined, though sometimes only temporarily, by others, many of whom were to become famous – Federn, Rank, Ferenczi, Sachs, and Hugo Heller, Freud's future publisher. Among early guests were Karl Abraham, who had a psychoanalytical practice in Berlin and became one of Freud's closest friends, A. A. Brill, Ernest Jones, Jung and Max Eitingon, also from Berlin and also to become an intimate friend.

In 1906, when Freud was fifty, his group of adherents presented him with a medallion. On one side was his profile and on the other a Greek design of Oedipus answering the sphinx. Around it is the line from Sophocles' *Oedipus Tyrannus*, 'Who was a man of very great powers, and saw through the secret riddle'. When Freud read the inscription, he paled and asked who had thought of it. Federn admitted he had been responsible for the choice. Then Freud disclosed that as a student he used to stroll round the arcaded court of the university inspecting busts of former professors, and had had the fantasy not only of one day seeing his own bust there – which would have been quite an ordinary thing for an ambitious student to imagine – but that he had actually fantasied those very words which he now saw on the medallion!

By 1908 – the year in which the Vienna Psycho-Analytical Society came into being – Freud's private practice had increased to full-time work. The majority of his patients came from Eastern Europe: few were from Vienna. Freud looked back on these years as his most peaceful and productive, taken up with professional and literary work, and a weekly game of cards (tarock) on Saturday at his friend Königstein's house, after he had given his university lecture at the hospital.

He saw his own children at meal-times, on Sundays and during the long summer holidays, to which they all looked forward so greatly. Freud loved mountain scenery, and had a good head for heights. He was a tremendous walker, light, swift and tireless. He appears to have been an unusually affectionate and lenient father, preferring to allow both sons and daughters to develop with as little interference as possible – a characteristic in keeping with his findings about the effects of unnecessary restraint and criticism during a child's early life.

Minna Bernays, Freud's sister-in-law, must have been important in his intellectual life, for she and Fliess are mentioned as the only people who encouraged him and showed interest in his work during the last years of the nineteenth century. Also, Freud was supremely fortunate in his wife, to whom he was devoted and to whom he was known always to be faithful. It was possible to share with her a totally serene domestic life. Ernest Jones writes that the children can never remember anything resembling a 'scene' taking place, and although Freud described himself as 'a cheerful pessimist' he was an agreeable and amusing companion, seldom criticizing plans laid before him.

His time-table gives some idea of the fullness and the orderliness of his life during the first fourteen years of this century. His first patient arrived at eight and so he had to be roused at seven, which was not always easy, since he seldom went to bed before one or two in the morning. He saw each patient for fifty-five minutes, taking five minutes off between each to refresh himself with a visit into the main part of the family apartment, which was adjacent to the separate office flat. If you go to Vienna now you will see a plaque at 19 Berggasse indicating that Freud lived and worked there. The family always lived on the first floor, but Freud's first office was at street level, his chair facing towards the garden at the back.

The main meal of the day was family lunch; at this he

talked little. If a child were absent, Freud would point silently to the empty place and direct an inquiring look at his wife. She would then explain the reason why the child had not appeared. A visitor present at the meal would find that the conversation with the family rested almost entirely with him, Freud being, no doubt, immersed in thoughts about the morning's work.

After lunch he would take a walk in the city, stopping daily to replenish his stock of cigars at a special *Tabak Trafik*. At 3 p.m. there would be consultations, and then further patients until 9 or even 10 p.m. He allowed himself no break before suppertime until he was 65, when he had a 5 o'clock cup of coffee. After a late supper, at which he would be more communicative, he would retire to his study to write his many letters (always by hand), correct proofs and see to new editions.

Of course the routine varied sometimes. The Wednesday Society met weekly, and every other Tuesday he attended the B'nai B'rith Society, the Jewish club or lodge to which he belonged, where he sometimes gave a paper. Saturdays were sacred to tarock. On Sundays he visited his mother. He seldom went to the theatre unless there was a Shakespeare play or a Mozart opera, but he was keen that the children should go, and would arrange to meet his daughters at a certain lamp-post to escort them home.

Freud maintained there were three things on which one should never economize: health, education and travel. He attempted to spare his young family the anxiety and trouble of hearing about money. His plan was that they should have everything they wanted for pleasure and education till they could earn their own living, and that after that they were to expect nothing. Though by no means a demonstrative man, Freud was the epitome of considerateness and wise affection. He loved giving presents, and would do so to special friends from his beloved collection of Greek, Assyrian and Egyptian antiquities, which was a source of particular interest and pleasure to him all his life. He could seldom wait for the exact date of a birthday, and the present would often arrive for a child the evening before.

He was an omnivorous sightseer, and regarded his visit

to Rome in 1901 with his brother Alexander as 'the high point in my life'. For years he had had a longing to go there, and it played an extensive part in his dream life. He described it as being 'the symbol for a number of warmly cherished wishes'. He knew, of course, that these must be based on desires belonging to early childhood, and at every visit to Rome he experienced great happiness and exaltation; yet there must also have been a mysterious taboo attached to it, for his earlier travels in northern and central Italy had brought him as far as Trasimeno (in 1897), and no farther. Was it a feared object as well as a wish fulfilment? It seems that he identified himself with the Semitic Hannibal and his attempt to gain possession of the 'Mother of Cities'. Freud readily admitted his love for ancient Rome, in whose history and culture he was steeped, and a fierce antagonism to the Christian Rome which had supplanted the ancient, and from which had sprung the age-long persecution of Jews. Even after he reached Rome, Freud related how his pleasure had been diminished by the evidence round him of what he called 'the lie of salvation'. From the dreams that he published, it becomes clear that his half-brother Emmanuel's immigration to England, which took place when Freud was three, left a very deep impression. Not only was part of his family leaving the birthplace, the old town, but they were leaving it because they belonged to a hated race and were going elsewhere to a different people, who were more tolerant, more loving. Did Rome represent two opposites for Freud's infantile unconscious – life among the older generation, with rigorous moral teachings, and his half-brother's freedom, independence and superiority in moving away from the parental country? However beloved one's parents and first family, the need to be one's own master, to be inner and not outer directed, exists in us all.

In August 1902, again with Alexander, Freud visited Venice and Naples, climbed Vesuvius and saw Pompeii, Capri and Paestum. In 1904 they both set out for Greece. From Brindisi to Patras they travelled with Professor Dorpfeld, the assistant to the famous archaeologist Schliemann. Freud is said to have gazed with awe at the man who had helped to discover ancient Troy, but was too

72

shy to approach him. Athens, with its wealth of classical lore and learning, was bound to overwhelm him. Twenty years later he said that the amber-coloured columns on the Acropolis were the most beautiful things he ever saw in his life. In a letter to Romain Rolland, he analysed the curious psychological experience he had while standing near the Parthenon. It was a peculiar sensation of utter disbelief in the reality of what was before his eyes. He puzzled Alexander by asking if it was true that they were on the Acropolis. Freud traced this incredulity to a psychological return to his student years. Then the idea of being in a position where he could visit such a wonderful place would have seemed incredible, and in turn would have been connected with the unconscious forbidden wish to excel his father. He compared the mechanism at work in himself at that moment as being operative in all those people who cannot tolerate success.

The gradual spread of knowledge of Freud's ideas, the application of his theories to the treatment of mentally disturbed people, led to his being recognized internationally. Inevitably, however, there was still an immense amount of opposition. Not only were people then, as they are now to a large degree, unwilling to contemplate mental disorder and its causes; theories about the relationship between emotion and thought and the importance of childhood experiences were unpalatable for much the same reasons as Darwin's theories had been. Most men, priding themselves upon their intellectual attainments and upon civilization as a whole, have little desire to study instinctual activities or the means whereby civilization comes about, nor do they want to realize the price paid for it in terms of repressions, inhibitions, etc. Nevertheless, among those professionally concerned, recognition of the importance of Freud's discoveries was growing steadily.

In 1895 F. W. H. Myers, of the Society for Psychical Research, was the first to lecture and write on *Studies on Hysteria* in London, only three months after it was published. In Zurich, by 1904, C. G. Jung and Eugen Bleuler, who was Professor of Psychiatry, had begun to study psychoanalysis and find various applications for it. Jung devised ingenious association tests, confirming Freud's

73

conclusions about the way in which emotional factors can interfere with recollection. Here the word *complex* was first incorporated into analytic jargon, being used when these tests showed up the presence of some repressed material. In 1906 a regular correspondence began between Freud and Jung which lasted for nearly seven years. To have his theories accepted in the Burghöltzli, the well-known mental hospital in Zurich, warmed Freud's heart, and he also very much liked Jung himself, at one time calling him his 'son and heir'.

Freud said that the first time he had a foretaste of becoming really famous was in 1908 when, on the way to America to lecture, he found his cabin steward reading *The Psychopathology of Everyday Life*. Ernest Jones had lectured and held several colloquiums in Yale and Harvard and had met many American psychiatrists, so when Freud was deliberating what to lecture about in the USA Jones was able to persuade him not to restrict himself to the subject of dreams, but to give a more general account of psychoanalysis. When the doctorate of Clark University, Worcester, was conferred on him he was visibly moved, and in his expression of thanks said, 'This is the first official recognition of our endeavours'. William James followed Freud's lectures with interest, and his parting words to Freud and Jones were, 'The future of psychology belongs to your work'. Freud describes in his autobiography a walk with James which made an indelible impression on him. James stopped suddenly, handed Freud the bag he was carrying and asked him to walk on, saying that he would catch Freud up as soon as he had got over an attack of angina pectoris, which was just coming on. He died of it later that year. Freud wrote how he always wished to be as fearless as that in the face of an approaching death.

The three friends and colleagues with whom Freud kept up a permanent correspondence and affectionate relationship were Abraham, Ferenczi and Jones. In 1904 Abraham had sent Freud a reprint of the first of his many valuable contributions to psychoanalysis. In 1907, after three years with Jung at Zurich, he decided to settle in Berlin and practise psychoanalysis there. Ferenczi, who lived in

Budapest, was a general practitioner who had experimented with hypnotism. In some measure he replaced Fliess. He spent holidays with Freud, and between 1908 and 1933 they exchanged more than a thousand letters in which a number of important psychoanalytic conclusions were clarified.

Ernest Jones was the only Briton and the only Gentile among the close colleagues round Freud. He wrote that as a Welshman he could sympathize with an oppressed race, and that he found it easy to remember the multitude of Jewish wise sayings and jokes. He was responsible for so much of the help and protection afforded to Freud that we owe him a very great debt of gratitude. Apart from this, his own contributions to psychoanalytic thought merit careful study. His long and detailed biography of Freud will go down in history as a model; few lives of great men have ever given such a fair and balanced picture without losing warmth and spontaneity.

In 1907 Max Eitingon, who was at that time a medical student, came to Vienna for three weeks to consult Freud about a severe case, and it was in this way that the first training analysis and supervision [sic] took place during a few evenings on long walks in the city. (Nowadays a student may expect to spend between five and six years before supervision ceases.) Hanns Sachs of Vienna had already attended Freud's lectures for several years, and Otto Rank, who came to Freud with an introduction from Adler, had joined the inner circle in 1906. This completed the six who in 1912 took it upon themselves to constitute a 'committee' to be responsible for the preservation and continuation of Freud's work, and to protect psychoanalysis and Freud himself from dissension. It was Jones who proposed the formation of this inner committee, suggesting that there should be only one definite obligation undertaken among them. This was that if anyone wished to depart from any of the fundamental tenets of psychoanalytical theory – e.g. the conception of the unconscious, of repression and of infantile sexuality – he would promise not to do so publicly before first discussing his views with the rest of them.

7 Dissensions – *Totem and Taboo*

To understand the need for such a protective measure, it is necessary to touch on the dissensions and desertions which psychoanalysis had to withstand during the three years before the first world war. Such dissensions really point to a stage of growth and strength which, with hindsight, one can see was inevitable. The movement now numbered approximately ninety members, all people of exceptional ability and intellect, coming from at least a dozen countries. They were all still beginners in a relatively little-known field of research and it would have been stultifying if there had been nothing but agreement among them. However, each schism and split shook the movement and caused a great deal of heartache at the time.

Alfred Adler and Wilhelm Stekel, who had been among the earliest of Freud's followers, both suffered from feelings of sibling rivalry in the face of Freud's undisguised preference for Jung, the foreigner. Both men seemed to feel that Freud's insistence on the basic tenets of psychoanalysis was strict and authoritarian. Freud himself was far from being an authoritarian person, but when it came to his findings and the theoretical and technical principles of psychoanalysis he stood firm. No one would claim that he did not take to heart the criticisms and obloquy which the world directed at him from 1905 onwards, but he realized that these were to be expected, for in the consulting room he had for years recognized resistance to interpretations about the unconscious. He fully understood, and stated, that 'the *odium sexicum* had replaced the *odium theologicum* of earlier epochs'. Being able to observe and understand the inbuilt fear and horror of sex which was present in so many men and women of those days, he was free of the resentment which others might have felt at being so often described as wicked and obsessed by sex. But radical criticisms, or the discarding of

76

basic findings, distressed him when they came from those who had first accompanied him into the arenas of international psychological and psychiatric debate.

The first deserter was Adler, who attributed to the will to power all aspects of personality and behaviour. He it was who coined the phrases, eventually to become so popular, 'inferiority complex' and 'masculine protest', and he concentrated on sociological and conscious phenomena rather than on repressions in the unconscious. Freud discussed Adler's ideas with the utmost seriousness and patience, but eventually came to the conclusion that they were 'scientific errors due to false methods – but still honourable errors', and that 'although one rejects the content of Adler's views, one can recognize their consistency and significance'.

In 1911 Adler and Stekel resigned their positions as, respectively, President and Vice-President of the Wednesday Society, and later that year Adler, at Freud's suggestion, ceased to be co-editor of the *Zentralblatt*, the newly formed publication started by the International Psycho-Analytical Association to keep the scattered analysts informed of each other's thought and experience.

Stekel had an unusual flair for detecting repressed material, and contributed a vast amount to our knowledge of symbolism. Freud felt that he possessed more intuitive genius than he had himself, but unfortunately he was lacking in any critical powers, and was more interested in producing an effect through his writings than in communicating truths. Unlike Adler he was an amusing, gay person. Freud said of him, 'He is only a trumpeter, but still I am fond of him'. He once had to refuse to publish material of Stekel's after he had admitted to making up part of it, and he knew, of course, from his analysis of Stekel how often this gifted man lied (which demonstrated to Freud Stekel's complete absence of scientific conscience).

The break came about in 1912 as the result of a dispute over the reviewing section of the *Zentralblatt*. Stekel was unwilling to accept a rebuke from Freud. His success in the field of symbolism made him feel he had surpassed Freud, and he often quoted in a half-modest manner that a dwarf on the head of a giant could see further than the giant himself. When Freud heard this he said, 'That may be so, but a louse on the head of an astronomer does not'. Stekel resigned from the Vienna Society in November 1911. Freud wrote to Abraham, 'How I have suffered from the labour of having to defend him against the whole world.'

The break with Jung was of a much more serious nature, for Freud had built high hopes on him and had seen him as his direct successor. The relationship between the two men had begun with the strongest possible mutual admiration. Freud was fascinated by Jung's vitality, and said that among the early analysts only Jung and Otto Gross – a brilliant psychiatrist who later developed schizophrenia – had original minds. Jung admired Freud's acumen and lucidity, though he had little or no regard for his followers. Jung's psychiatric training, and his devotion to the work, made his choice as president of the International Psycho-Analytical Association obvious, but he had an inner need to align himself with a younger generation, to rebel against authority (e.g. father figures), which prevented him from being content to cast in his lot with the existing founders of an association established before his arrival on the scene. Neither Freud nor Jung himself faced up sufficiently to this urge of Jung's to rebel.

From 1909 onwards it slowly became apparent that both in theoretical beliefs and in practice with patients Jung was avoiding commitment to the concept of sexual aetiology, both in the neuroses and in the explanation of human development. At the end of 1910, at a friendly meeting in Munich, Freud bade him, 'Return in good time to the neuroses – the motherland where we have first to fortify our dominion against everything and everybody'. This was apropos Jung's interest and brilliance in investigating the realms of mythology and the history of mankind, which, though equally fascinating to Freud, could only be regarded by him as 'colonies of psychoanalysis'. Jung had previously admitted to Jones that he found it unnecessary to go into details of 'unsavoury topics' with his patients, and to Abraham that he thought 'we should do well not to burst out with the theory of sexuality in the foreground'. Freud was distressed at reports from Switzerland that mythological researches interfered with Jung's work as

President of the International Psycho-Analytical Association, but even more upset by the news that all the Swiss analysts had abandoned the sexual theories in the face of the practical and moral difficulties surrounding them in their country, where the Press published articles daily denouncing 'the wickedness coming from Vienna'.

In 1911 Frau Jung mentioned in a letter her fear that Freud would not like what her husband was writing in the second part of his essay about *libido* (the term which analysts use for the fund of energy in each individual). She was right. Jung was now stating his view that the Freudian idea that incest wishes are universal in every unconscious should not be taken literally but only as a 'symbol of higher ideas'. Then in 1912 there were reports that Jung, who was then in New York, was making antagonistic and critical remarks about Freud. On his return he sent a long account of how successful he had been in making psychoanalysis more acceptable in America through leaving out the sexual theme. Freud replied tersely that there was nothing clever in this; if one left out more it would become still more acceptable. But as late as September that year Freud expressed the hope that their former personal relationship could be restored and a separation be avoided.

In November, when they met again at Munich, Jung promised to reform, after Freud had helped him to see some of his personal and unconscious reactions in 'everyday life pathologies'. One of these had been his failure to check the date of a postmark on a letter from Freud, inviting him to a meeting which he had overlooked; he had felt injured about this for six months. After this talk Freud felt that he had won him back to the fold and was elated. It is clear that Jung symbolized for him a much greater challenge than anyone else. Twice he fainted when Jung was present, each time after he had been successful in persuading Jung to change his views – once at this meeting in Munich, the other time in 1909, when he changed Jung's attitude to alcohol. Analysing the second faint, which Ferenczi had thought might occur as a repetition of the first, Freud believed that it had to do with the traumatic effect upon him of his baby brother's death. At that time he would have had the unconscious fantasy that an opponent

79

was defeated as a result of unconscious death wishes. Jones regarded the fainting episodes as confirmation that Freud was unable to tolerate success, and saw both faints as symptoms in the same category as the bewilderment felt on the Acropolis, which Freud traced as resulting from a realization of the forbidden wish to excel his father.

After the 1912 meeting Jung returned from Munich to Zurich and wrote an apologetic letter assuring Freud of his loyalty. This, however, lasted no time. On being reminded that some of his ideas about the incest complex resembled Adler's, Jung wrote angrily, 'Not even Adler's companions think that I belong to *your* group', when he really meant to write *their*. (This slip of the pen is easier to make in German as it only involves using a capital letter instead of a small one.) Freud inquired if he, Jung, were sufficiently objective to look into the error. It was an unwise question to ask of someone in such a sensitive mood as Jung was then in: Freud got what he was probably unconsciously asking for – an insolent reply.

Thereafter the two corresponded only on business matters, and even this soon ceased. Analysts had reason to wonder whether the Association could survive such a split. Freud himself wrote, 'Naturally everything that tries to get away from our truths will find approval among the general public. Possibly this time we shall really be buried after the burial hymn has so often been sung over us in vain. That will change a great deal in our personal fate but nothing in that of Science. We possess the truth; I am as sure of it as fifteen years ago. I have never taken part in polemics, my habit is to repudiate in silence and go my own way.'

Maeder wrote to Ferenczi that the scientific differences between the Viennese and the Swiss were due to the former being Jews, the latter Aryans. Freud advised Ferenczi to say that this difference in outlook and in art could be seen every day but that there could be no such thing as Aryan or Jewish science. Scientific results had to be identical though presentation of them might vary.

Two-fifths of the 1913 Congress abstained from voting in favour of Jung's re-election as president.[1] That was in

[1] Annual congresses of the International Association had been held since 1909.

80

September. In October he resigned his editorship of the *Jahrbuch*, and announced that no further cooperation with Freud was possible. In April 1914 he also resigned his presidency, probably because of the number of adverse reviews about him. Just before the first world war broke out the Swiss analysts let it be known that none of them would attend the next Congress. Freud realized only too well what such a break with them would mean. 'Anyone,' he wrote in a letter to Jones, 'who promises to mankind liberation from the hardships of sex will be hailed as a hero – let him talk whatever nonsense he chooses.' And this prediction was soon proved true. Only a few months afterwards the *British Medical Journal* hailed Jung's conversion as 'a return to a saner view of life'. Psychologists were glad to point out that now there were three schools of psychoanalysis – Freud, Adler and Jung – and since they could not agree about their own data there was no real need for anyone else to take the subject seriously.

But a firm foundation of understanding had been built up by the International Association. There were the annual congresses, while the *Zentralblatt* and the *Jahrbuch* kept the alert members of the medical profession and every analyst informed as to the current thought and practice in the new science. The national societies or sub-groups,[1] developed at different rates. There was one in Berlin, one in Zurich, later one in Budapest. In America Jones influenced Dr James Putnam, Professor of Neurology at Harvard, to found a society where psychoanalytical ideas could be discussed even though some of the members were not analysts; this, the American Psychopathological Association, was born in 1910. Forty members attended the first meeting, so great was the interest stirred up by the lectures given at Worcester by Freud, Jung and Jones.

A special periodical *Psychotherapia*, was founded in Moscow, and reviews about psychoanalysis appeared there. Italy was much more involved in the movement than France. For a while both Australia and Canada had small societies. Whenever he could, Jones saw to it that the findings of psychoanalysis were known about in England,

[1] Each member was also a member of the International Association.

but even as late as 1911 an audience of eight left the room when M. D. Eder reached the sexual aetiology in a paper which he was reading to the neurological section of the British Medical Association.

Freud's writings about the psychology of love and narcissism (1910), his case history about five-year-old Hans, whose terror of horses was treated by means of consultations between Freud and the father, his founding of yet another journal, *Imago*, devoted to non-medical aspects of psychoanalysis – all this indicated his belief that analysis was not just a tool to relieve immediate mental ill-health. Between 1913 and 1914 he wrote *Totem and Taboo*, which linked anthropological material to his theories. He described his reactions while he was putting this important book together. 'The Totem work is a beastly business. I am reading thick books without being really interested in them, since I already know the results. My instinct tells me that. But it has to slither its way through all the material on the subject. In this process one's insight gets clouded – there are many things that don't fit yet mustn't be forced. I haven't time every evening, and so on. With all that I feel as if I had intended only to start a little liaison and then discovered at my time of life I have to marry a new wife!' Later he said of the book, 'I have not written anything with so much conviction since *The Interpretation of Dreams*'. At that time he felt it to be his 'greatest and perhaps last good work'. He told Abraham that the essay would appear before the Munich Congress and would 'serve to make a sharp division between us and all Aryan religiosity'.

When the work was finished he was elated, but this was soon replaced by doubt and misgiving. However, Jones and Ferenczi read the proofs together in Budapest and wrote to him in high praise. Later that month, in Vienna, Jones asked how the man who had written *The Interpretation of Dreams* could now have such doubts. Freud replied, 'Then I described the wish to kill one's father. Now I have been describing the actual killing. After all, it is a big step from a wish to a deed.'

The first part of *Totem and Taboo* concerns the horror of incest and notes all the precautions which primitive

82

tribes take to guard against it. Freud inferred that the temptation was greater with such tribes and that they could not, as civilized people do, rely on deeply organized repressions. Thus the latter could be compared to neurotics who established complicated phobias or symptoms which serve the same purpose as taboos serve for these tribes. Freud went on to liken the ancient taboos to the *délire de toucher* (compulsion to touch) often seen in people suffering from some obsessional neurosis. He drew certain parallels between a primitive taboo system and modern obsessions: the lack of any conscious motive; the feeling of great compulsion to observe the system; the capacity of the taboo to become displaced; the ceremonial designed to undo the dreaded harm.

That the ceremony involves as a rule some kind of deprivation led Freud to think that the taboos themselves meant renunciation of something that was tempting but had become forbidden. Freud felt that the temptations in the neuroses were usually of a sexual kind, but that in the case of the primitive taboos the concern was with various anti-social impulses – mainly aggression and murder. He wrote, 'The neuroses display striking resemblances to the great social productions of art, religion and philosophy, and in fact appear as caricatures of them. Hysteria the caricature of an artistic creation, obsessional neurosis a caricature of religion, and paranoid delusions a caricature of a philosophical system.' The third part of *Totem and Taboo* deals with animism, magic and the omnipotence of thoughts. Freud was able to illustrate a direct correlation between primitive belief in magic and neurotic fantasies and the mental life of very young children.

The fourth part is entitled 'The Infantile Return of Totemism'. This begins by elaborating the theme of protection from incest when a totem animal or plant can represent a clan or tribe and facilitates the demarcation of marriage permissions. Freud agreed with Darwin's supposition that early man must have lived, as do the higher apes, in small hordes consisting of one powerful male and several females. He assumed from this that the growing sons, debarred from the females, would periodically band together and slay and devour the father. He postulated that this would lead to ambivalence, feelings of love and hate towards the father, remorse and rivalry among the brothers, and from this a return to obedience to a father's rule, including the barrier against incest.

Freud refers to Robertson Smith's writings about sacrifice and sacrificial feasts, where the totem is ceremonially slain and eaten; in this way the original murder is repeated, followed first by mourning and then by rejoicing. From this the permanent community, through individual and group experience, continuously absorbs and reabsorbs the virtues of the great ancestor. After thousands of years the totem becomes a god and the history of religion begins. Freud reminds readers that early Greek tragedy contained a hero who, despite warnings from a chorus, pursues a forbidden path to his doom. He describes this as a 'hypocritical inversion', meaning that the chorus symbolizes the rebel brothers and the hero the victim. Towards the end of the book there is a notable sentence which runs, 'The beginnings of religion, morality, social life and art meet in the Oedipus complex'. Lastly, he states that social development could well have been stimulated by reactions of guilt to the murderous wishes alone, since in the infantile unconscious the wish and the deed are one – there is no intermediate state or pause for reflection. He concludes, 'In the beginning was the deed'.

Although this book was badly received outside analytic circles ('just one more personal fantasy of Freud's'), the interest in psychoanalysis grew. In February 1914 a reprint came from Holland showing that the Rector of Leyden University supported Freud's theory of dreams and had referred to it sympathetically in an address at the 339th Anniversary of the Founding. Freud was pleased, and wrote, 'Just think, an official psychiatrist and Rector of a University swallows psychoanalysis skin and hair – what more surprises can we expect!' But little triumphs like this could not offset his disappointment when Stanley Hall, the President of Clark University, Worcester, who had done so much to make psychoanalysis known in the United States, decided to become known as a follower of Adler. Later he wrote very handsome tributes to Freud, but nothing could mend the effect of this sort of defection.

8 The First World War and After

Freud's knowledge of human beings did not, apparently, enable him to make more perspicacious political judgements than anyone else. He expected 'bad times', as he said in a letter written in 1912; but the outbreak of war was as much a surprise to him as to other Austrians. Jones commented, 'One would have supposed that a pacifist *savant* of fifty-eight would have greeted it with simple horror – as so many did – but his first response was one of youthful enthusiasm – a re-awakening of the military ardours of his boyhood.' Freud wrote at the outbreak, 'I should be with it with all my heart if only I could think England would not be on the wrong side.' But he soon gained a wiser perspective, and gave up any hope of a rapid end to the war.

During the first months he experienced one of his great spells of productivity. Not only did he manage to keep the psychoanalytic periodicals going – the *Zeitschrift* and the *Imago* – but in six weeks during the spring of 1915 he wrote five essays which contain some of his most profound thinking. *Instincts and Their Vicissitudes* and *Repression* took three weeks. His favourite, *The Unconscious*, took a fortnight, and in eleven days he completed *The Metapsychological Supplement to the Theory of Dreams* and *Mourning and Melancholia*.

The following six weeks saw five more essays written, and in August he wrote to Jones that all twelve of the projected series were almost finished. He intended eventually to publish them in book form, but wrote, 'Now is not the time'. The last seven essays, in fact, never appeared in printed form. It is supposed that for some reason Freud became dissatisfied with this summing up of his life's work, and destroyed the essays when further ideas began to emerge which would have meant completely re-casting these writings.

During 1915 Otto Rank, who had been helping with the editorial work and the cataloguing of the library which the Vienna Society had been collecting since 1908, was called up, as was Sachs. Ferenczi was serving as a doctor in the Hungarian Hussars. Freud saw few analytic friends, but some of his letters continued to reach them, and a number got through to him from Jones and Abraham and a few other friends. Phrases from these indicate the sadness, tension and loneliness which these years brought to them all. During the first October of the war he had no patients, and wrote that he had the full leisure in his study for which he had often longed. He added wryly, 'That's what fulfilled wishes look like!'

To his well-known pupil, Lou Andreas-Salomé, he wrote, 'I do not doubt that mankind will surmount even this war, but I and my contemporaries will never again see a joyous world.' In the same letter he continued, 'My secret conclusion was: since we can only regard the highest civilization of the present as disfigured by gigantic hypocrisy, it follows that we are organically unfitted for it. We have to abdicate and the Great Unknown He or It lurking behind Fate will some time repeat such an experiment with another race.'

Letters between him and Ferenczi dealt with much of what he later wrote about the conscious and the unconscious. In one of them his gloom about the immediate outlook for psychoanalysis in the current state of the world is shown by the remark, 'What Jung and Adler have left of the movement is being ruined by the strife of nations'. It was at this time that he decided to give up his annual university lectures. Everything seemed to him to be closing down. *Thoughts for the Times on War and Death*, which he wrote then, has often been reprinted, and should be read by everyone.

During 1916 several of his letters mention the food shortage, influenza and the many signs of recognition at the time of his sixtieth birthday. 1917 proved still more dismal. He wrote of the First Russian Revolution, 'How much one would have entered into this tremendous change if our first consideration were not one of peace!' Later he wrote to Ferenczi that he felt sure there would be no hope of peace till the Americans arrived. He had by then lost all sympathy with Germany, though he said he cared little for the other side. Writing to Abraham, he said he could hardly imagine travelling to Germany even when it became possible; that, like Donna Blanca in Heine's poem 'Disputation in Toledo', 'All I can say is that both parties stink'. The only cheerful news, he continued, was the capture of Jerusalem by the English, and their proposal to turn it into a home for the Jews.

Ferenczi and Anton von Freund, a rich Budapest brewer of whom Freud and Ferenczi became very fond, managed to smuggle flour and a few luxuries to the Freud family from Hungary by various complicated manœuvres. So did the brother of an ex-patient in Holland. Freud's study was unheated, and letters could only be written with freezing fingers; scientific writing was considered an impossibility during the winter months. At this time too, he was troubled by rheumatism and prostate trouble; yet, after mentioning these facts, Freud adds, 'Curiously enough I am quite well, my spirits unshaken. It is proof of how little justification in reality one needs for inner well-being.'

He spent a summer holiday that year 4000 feet up in Csorbató. It was cold and stormy, but he was able to walk there, and he enjoyed finding mushrooms. Ferenczi and Sachs stayed with him, and Eitingon and Rank also managed a few days there. His practice was naturally variable. That year it started with no patients, improved in April, but narrowed down to three in June, which gives an indication of his ability to use analytic technique with patients when there was no prospect of a long analysis.

In the spring of 1917 Freud wrote a paper called, *A Difficulty in the Path of Psychoanalysis*. It sketched out three blows which science had administered to man's pride. He had discovered that his earth was not the centre of the universe; that he was evolved from the animal kingdom; and that he was not even master of his own mind. Freud also finished the *Introductory Lectures*, the first part of which he had published in 1915, and in the train on the journey back from Csorbató he wrote a little paper on Goethe. But his thoughts that year were mainly centred on the project which he wanted to undertake with Ferenczi – a consideration of the bearing that Lamarckism had on psychoanalysis. Lamarck was a well-known French naturalist of the eighteenth century who had framed his own 'laws'. The second of them concerns the growth of a certain organ in an animal as a direct result of that genus of animal needing such an organ. The fourth law states that 'acquired characteristics can be inherited'. Freud wrote, 'Our intention is to show that his, Lamarck's, "need", which creates and transforms organs, is nothing other than the power of unconscious ideas over the body of which we see relics in hysteria.' Freud went on to state that two great principles of change and progress would then be seen, one autoplastic, through the adaptation of one's own body, and a later one, heteroplastic, through the transmutation of the outer world.

Although it was not recognized as such at the time, the first signs of cancer made their appearance on Freud's palate at the end of this year. The connexion with smoking is in his case unmistakable. He had been going very short of his beloved cigars, and when he had smoked his last, noticed how very tired and bad-tempered he felt. He had palpitations, and a worsening of the painful swelling in the palate which had appeared 'since the straitened days. Then a patient brought me fifty cigars, I lit one, became cheerful, and the affection of the palate went down. I should not have believed it if it had not been so striking.' That was six years before the real cancer attacked him in that place. Nowadays surgeons often refer to a precancerous stage. It is doubtful whether anyone could have helped Freud through his dependence on nicotine. In any case, it would have been virtually impossible for another analyst to have exercised the authority or commanded the transference feelings necessary for such help to be effective. Nowadays such dependency can sometimes be relieved through psychoanalysis, a fact which somehow makes Freud's subsequent cancer and pain of singular dramatic irony.

In 1918, during the German offensive, he wrote, 'I suppose we have to wish for a German victory. That is (1) a displeasing idea and (2) still improbable.' It is interesting to note such a careless way of writing from someone whose main output was usually so meticulously clear and well defined, an example of the *schlamperei* which he had confessed to in early days. Clear-sightedness and blind spots with regard to his own emotional reactions were both illustrated that year in letters to Abraham. 'My alternation of courage and resignation takes shelter in your even temperament and indestructible sense of vitality.' Three months later, 'My mother will be eighty-three this year. Sometimes I think I shall feel a little freer when she dies, for the idea that she might have to be told I had died is a terrifying thought.'

His friend, Anton von Freund, had been operated on for cancer, and had become neurotic through apprehension of a recurrence; Freud treated him for his neurosis with success. Gratitude urged von Freund to use his fortune for the furtherance of psychoanalysis, and Ferenczi and Freud, with Rank's subsequent help, decided to found a publishing firm of their own, which they called the *Verlag*. This would free them from the frequent difficulties they had encountered with Heller, Freud's publisher, which were not by any means only to do with shortages of paper and print. The second pleasant event was the Fifth International Congress in September. The energetic Abraham arranged for it to take place in Budapest, which Freud then declared to be 'the centre of the psychoanalytic movement'.

This was the first Congress graced by government officials, representing Austria, Germany and Hungary. They attended because of the increasing realization of the importance which war neuroses played in military strategy, and their presence was a mark of recognition of the work performed in this sphere by Abraham, Eitingon and Ferenczi. High-ranking army officials began to talk of establishing psychoanalytic clinics at various centres. Ferenczi was chosen as the next President of the International Association, special receptions and dinners were given, and in the following month more than a thousand students petitioned the Rector of the University that Ferenczi should be invited to give a course of lectures there. Freud, who usually spoke without using any notes, for some reason read his paper at the Congress. It was entitled 'Lines of Advance in Psychoanalytic Therapy'.

Although as far as possible he kept aloof from the formal ceremonies, he was moved by the sudden bright prospects for the extension of his work. He wrote that his heart was light to think of his *Sorgenkind* (child of cares) protected by Ferenczi and the others.

His friend and colleague, Pfister, published a new book in October, and their correspondence reopened. Freud praised it, but disagreed with Pfister's views on infantile sexuality and on ethics. He wrote of the latter, 'The topic lies far from my interest but you have the care of souls – I don't rack my brain much about the problem of good and evil, but on the whole I have not found much of the "good" in people'. He went on, 'From a therapeutic point of view, I can only envy you the possibility of sublimation that religion affords. But the beauty of religion certainly does not belong to the domain of psychoanalysis', and a little further on, 'By the way, how comes it that none of the pious people discovered psychoanalysis? Why did they have to wait for a quite godless Jew?'

From the middle of the war onwards Freud had had reason to fear that his financial circumstances might end in bankruptcy. However, his brother-in-law, Eli Bernays, sent him a considerable sum from New York before the Americans entered the war – a welcome recompense for Freud's help to him when he had emigrated a quarter of a century before.

The German downfall and the break-up of the Austro–Hungarian Empire saw Freud angry with President Wilson for misleading Europe when he made promises that he could not in any way fulfil. He wrote, 'The times are frightfully tense. It is a good thing that the old should die, but the new is not here yet. I shall weep not a single tear for the fate of Austria or Germany.'

For many weeks the family were without news of the eldest son, Martin, who was on active service, but on 3 December they got a postcard simply announcing his arrival in an Italian hospital. Both Martin and Ernst had spent the war in the army, while the third son, Oliver, was an engineer in government service. All came through safely. Anna, his youngest daughter, founded the Hampstead Clinic and has been one of London's foremost psychoanalysts for many years. She first qualified as a teacher, and her contributions to the analysis of children are world-famous.

Conditions during the interval between the armistice in November 1918 and the peace made in the following summer were very rigorous. Freud complained, 'All the four years of war were a joke compared with the bitter grimness of these months', and 'Now my capacity for adaptation (versus altering the outside world) is on strike. I remain ill-humoured and must avoid infecting other people when they are young and strong.'

The years that followed were dreadfully hard in Vienna. Freud treated patients, wearing a thick overcoat and gloves, hour after hour, and then with frozen fingers corrected the proofs of the numerous periodicals and new editions for which he was responsible. The steady rise in prices and the eventual inflation led to the loss of all his savings. He wrote to Ferenczi, 'What would happen to me if Jones were not able to send me patients?', for English and American patients paid him in dollars and pounds on which he could live.

Budding analysts also came from these countries in order to learn his technique. For Freud this was a considerable strain, since he found the different accents hard to follow. He wrote to Jones, 'You shall hear no complaints – I am still upright and hold myself not responsible for any part of the world's nonsense'. To Ferenczi, who was, with some reason, counting on official recognition in Hungary, he wrote, 'Keep a reserved attitude. We are not suited to any kind of official existence', and later in the same letter, 'We are and must remain far from any tendentiousness, except from the one aim of investigating and helping.' Nowadays it is to be debated whether orthodox psychoanalysts are right in adhering to this principle; some of them are suited to official existence, and the sooner practising analysts accept government, teaching and hospital posts the better.

In 1919 the British Psycho-Analytical Society was reorganized, and proper links with the British Psychological Society were formed through the special medical section founded by Ernest Jones and J. C. Flugel. In

Budapest Ferenczi was made first University Professor of Psychoanalysis; but when a reactionary régime supplanted the Bolsheviks he could hardly show his face with safety. Until the mid-1920s Freud was read and studied in Russia and analysts practised in Moscow and several other towns. Jones was surprised, when he met Freud in 1919, to hear that an ardent Communist had half-converted him. This man had told Freud that the advent of Bolshevism would result in some years of misery and chaos, but that these would be followed by universal peace, prosperity and happiness. Freud had said, however, that he believed the first half of this only.

The end of the war and the victory of the western powers made Freud realize that what he called 'the centre of gravity of psychoanalysis' would have to be moved. He and Ferenczi agreed to transfer to Jones the acting presidency of the International Association. He also suggested that Eitingon should join the private 'Committee', and the others at once agreed. The necessary insignia of a ring (Freud had given one to each member) was arranged. Later Freud gave his daughter, Anna, a similar ring. The only other women to receive this honour were Lou Salomé, Marie Bonaparte and Ernest Jones' wife, Katherine.

In 1919 Freud was made a full Professor of the University at Vienna, but this gave him neither a seat on the Board of Faculty nor any teaching duties.

1920 brought him two grievous losses. Anton von Freund, his friend and patient and the first great benefactor to psychoanalysis, died; and suddenly, five days later, his beautiful daughter Sophie – the one they called their 'Sunday child' – died of influenza, at her home in Hamburg at the age of twenty-six, leaving two young children. To Eitingon Freud wrote, 'It is a paralysing event', and, 'If one is not a believer one is spared all the conflicts which go with that. Blunt necessity, mute submission.' To Ferenczi he wrote, 'Quite deep down I can trace the feeling of a deep narcissistic hurt that is not to be healed. My wife and Anna are terribly shaken in a more human way.'

1920 also saw the founding of the Berlin Policlinic. For a long time this was the most famous training institute for psychoanalysis. The buildings were given by Eitingon, and the design was arranged by Freud's son Ernst. Hanns Sachs and Theodor Reik, an analyst from Vienna, taught there. This clinic fulfilled the post-war promise for his work which Freud longed to see. He did not feel that Vienna was a suitable centre, but a clinic, the Ambulatorium, was opened there in 1922.

Despite Freud's conviction that it was important to remain completely out of official undertakings, this was not always possible, as is shown by the history of the memorandum which he had to write on the electrical treatment of war neurotics. A special commission had been set up by the Austrian military to investigate complaints that some of the military doctors in the psychiatric department of the Vienna General Hospital had given their patients treatment which involved cruelty. Freud expressed his personal conviction that the director, Professor Wagner-Jauregg, would never have allowed the electrical dosage to be intensified to an inhuman pitch, but he could not vouch for the other doctors, whom he did not know. The report went on to point out that the brilliant initial successes of the treatment by means of strong electrical currents had proved not to be lasting. In his opinion, few soldiers were malingerers pure and simple. It was difficult to apply psychoanalysis in war-time to soldiers suffering from neuroses, but he believed that a knowledge of psychoanalytical principles would have been more useful than the electrical therapy. Through these principles would come more sympathy and an understanding of the nature of emotional conflict – in the case of war neuroses, between the instinct of self-preservation and the demands of duty.

Freud pointed out that in war-time there was a conflict for the doctor too, in so far as his duty demanded that he should put the patient's interests first, while the military authorities for whom he worked required the patient for active service.

9 Illness and the years of fame

In February 1923, when Freud was sixty-seven, he noticed a growth on the right side of his jaw and palate. He said nothing about this to anyone, but, having consulted two medical acquaintances, turned up in April at the out-patient department of the hospital where one of them worked, so that the growth could be removed. The operation, which he had been assured would be a slight one, did not go as expected. During the night there was severe bleeding, and it is possible that Freud's life was saved by the prompt action of the patient whose room he was sharing. His whole treatment on the occasion of this operation – the first of thirty-three – was extremely negligent. No precautions were taken against the shrinkage of the scar, so that great contraction took place which seriously reduced the opening of his mouth. He was given drastic radium treatment, and four months later he mentioned in a letter that he had not had an hour free from pain since the treatment ceased. He referred to a 'comprehensive indifference' in himself 'to most of the trivialities of life', for the physical shock was succeeded by an experience which, as he told Marie Bonaparte, he had found quite unbearable. His small grandson Heinerle, Sophie's second child, died of tuberculosis on 19 June. The child had been delicate, and had had his tonsils removed at the time of Freud's operation. There had been a very close bond between him and his grandfather. Freud maintained that he was the most intelligent child he had ever encountered.

In July he told Ernest Jones that he was suffering from the first real depression of his life, and maintained that 'the working through the mourning is going on in the depths'. Among the trivialities of life he counted science itself. 'I have no fresh ideas and have not written a line.' Later still he wrote that the loss of the little boy affected him quite differently from all others. 'Those,' he said, 'had brought about sheer pain, but this killed something in me for good.' He also observed that after this he was never able to get fond of anyone new, but merely retained his old attachments. To one old friend he wrote that Heinerle had stood to him for all children and grandchildren, and that since his death he had not been able to enjoy life, adding, 'It is the secret of my indifference – people call it courage – toward the danger of my own life.'

During his 1923 summer vacation he asked his friend, Felix Deutsch, to visit him. Deutsch, who was a surgeon, perceived a recurrence of the growth, necessitating a major operation, but delayed telling Freud the truth. There were perhaps some good reasons for this, though later Freud found them inadequate. Most of the Committee felt that Freud should be in possession of all the facts, but perhaps they all thought that he must be more or less aware of the situation.

The distinguished oral surgeon, Hans Pichler, was asked to take charge of Freud's case, and the operation took place in two stages on 4 and 11 October. It involved the ligaturing of the external carotid artery, the removal of the submaxillary glands, and the slitting of lip and cheek to remove the whole upper jaw and palate on the affected side. Freud could not speak, and had to be fed by nasal tube for some days, but he was allowed to return home on 28 October.

Sixteen years of discomfort and pain followed, with recurrences of the trouble and further operations. Freud had to wear a huge magnified denture called a prosthesis to shut off the mouth from the nasal cavity; this was known by the family as 'the monster'. It was difficult to fit in, but necessary in order to make eating and speaking possible. In the course of all this his Eustachian tube became damaged, so that he was virtually deaf on the right side, the side next to his patients. The position of his couch and chair therefore had to be reversed.

At the beginning Freud had made a pact with his daughter, Anna, that there would be no sentiment displayed between them. He would have no other nurse than her, and all that had to be done was performed in a cool, matter-of-fact fashion with a complete absence of emotion.

95

This, combined with her courage and firmness, enabled her to adhere to the pact despite many agonizing situations.

Freud resumed work with six patients in January 1924. He admitted to being very tired and in need of rest, but he wanted to go on earning, especially since his illness had cost a great deal. He always insisted on paying his doctors in full. New 'monsters' were made in the hope of getting something which suited him better, and smoking was allowed, though to get a cigar between his teeth he had to force the bite open with the help of a clothes-peg.

The news of his serious illness brought signs of friendliness from Vienna, and a title akin to the English 'freedom of the city' was bestowed on him. Freud regarded this ironically, and called it 'a ritual performance'.

Jones visited him in the spring of 1924; despite his altered appearance, the change in his voice and his habit of keeping the prosthesis in its place with his thumb, he found Freud as alert and mentally keen as ever. Accounts of the eighth International Congress relieved him, since he had feared that criticism of the activities of Ferenczi and Rank might provoke dissension or difficulty. Rank had elaborated a theory, and also a new 'short cut' treatment, in relation to the trauma of being born, and in doing so had disrupted the normal course of growth of psychoanalysis in America, where he had been invited by the New York Society. His behaviour had been thoroughly unreliable and very distressing indeed to Freud and to the Committee who had worked with him for many years. Ferenczi had joined with him in writing *The Development of Psycho-Analysis*, which had been criticized by the rest of the Committee, not only because it was published without prior consultation with them but also because, though it gave a brilliant account of how patients 'live out' or 'act out' their unconscious impulses, the technique recommended concentrated too much on the analysis of the 'here and now' situation and too little on the analysis of childhood.

By 1924 psychoanalysis was established in several capitals of Europe and in America. Analytic training institutes, such as that in Berlin, were being set up in Vienna, London and New York. That year Freud published five papers. One, 'The Economic Problem of Masochism', was

96

the outcome of further ideas about problems which had been discussed in *Beyond the Pleasure Principle* (first published in 1920.)

Perhaps more than in any other of his books one can see in *Beyond the Pleasure Principle* Freud's cool, clear, relaxed and supremely scientific mode of thought. One is shown how he conducted arguments, first with himself and then with colleagues. One gets a glimpse of the width of his reading in biology as well as among poets, philosophers and collectors of myths. He is at pains to explain what he means by a repetition compulsion, the unconscious drive which causes individuals to play and replay experiences that have been important to them – even the original traumata. In this book he describes his well-known observation of an eighteen-month-old boy who re-enacted his mother's daily departure by throwing small toys and objects away from him to places where they could not easily be seen, and later threw away and pulled back a cotton reel on a string, making sounds which meant 'gone' to him as he threw. Freud's hypothesis was that by seeming to master a painful situation (for this little boy it was separation from his mother), either by becoming the active person in the scene instead of the passive, or by making a game – a comedy – out of what could be felt as a tragedy, the repetition enabled the sufferer to assimilate and work through that first painful experience. He went on to describe how, as treatment proceeds in analysis, the patient unconsciously seeks to bring about repetitions of an original trauma, and from this becomes able to see and feel some of the strange motives in his unconscious which account for symptoms, characteristics and behaviour.

Concerning the patient's natural resistance to this liberation of repressed material Freud wrote, 'Our efforts are directed towards procuring the toleration of that unpleasure by appeal to the reality principle'. From here his reasoning moved on to claim that the purpose of a repetition compulsion is, as it were, to immunize the ego from the effects of the stimuli originally felt, insuring against the possibility of ever again being surprised and subjected to so much stimulation, and thereby proving it feasible to assimilate and withstand that particular experience. He added that it is for this reason that small children demand pleasurable experiences in their games and stories to be repeated without any alteration, for the mastery implicit in the exact recurrence enables them to feel in full possession of the enjoyable experience. They too 'play out' happenings that have been stressful and, just as adults enjoy dramatic performances with frightening or tragic plots, so children enjoy reading or pretending about hospital visits, operations, car accidents and so on.

It is in this book that Freud remarks, 'The indefiniteness of all our discussions on what we describe as metapsychology is of course due to the fact that *we know nothing of the nature of the exciting process* that takes place in the elements of the psychical systems, and that we do not feel justified in framing any hypothesis on the subject. We are consequently operating all the time with a large unknown quantity which we are obliged to carry over into every new formula.'

The absence of exact knowledge about excitory processes continues to render all professional psychologists tentative. Freud was no exception; but his hypotheses were so ingenious and so often plausible that a common reaction is either to applaud all of them too readily or to criticize too destructively.

Having stressed the difference between what he calls the primary processes of unconscious life and the secondary processes in 'normal waking life', Freud ends the book with a debate about the death instinct. He considers the proposition that there is in any organism a greater inborn propensity for conservatism, for resisting change and development, and restoring an earlier state of things, than there is drive to make changes. He investigates the idea that death is inevitable wherever there is reproduction, and supports a view of the dualistic nature of libido which he thought contained two instincts, Eros and Thanatos. This concept is continually discussed among psychologists, many of whom prefer to think of libido as unified and death as merely a cessation of the life force. Freud points out in this respect that, whereas his extension of the concept of sexuality and his hypothesis of narcissism were based on observed phenomena, 'It is impossible to pursue

an idea of this kind [the death instinct] except by re-
peatedly combining factual material with what is purely
speculative and thus diverging widely from observation'.
He went on to say later, 'It should be made quite clear that
the uncertainty of our speculation has been greatly increased by the necessity for borrowing from the science of
biology. *Biology is truly a land of unlimited possibilities.*' He
never ceased to stress his belief that one day most of his
theory would become explicable, and be superseded, by
physiological and chemical knowledge.

This day, as yet, looks a very long way off. What he
could hardly have guessed was that lengthy, scientific
studies made of animal behaviour – such, for instance, as
those conducted by Sir Julian Huxley, Eliot Howard,
Timbergen and Lorenz, and described by Robert Ardrey –
would so greatly enlarge the psychoanalyst's horizon as
well as that of the experimental psychologist. He would
undoubtedly have been foremost in acclaiming the value of
such research, and perhaps would have been able to bring
about a more effective and creative *entente* than at present
exists between animal and human studies.

It is here that one must also remember the mystical
aspect of Freud which led him to write to Jones, after
reading about Gilbert Murray's telepathy experiments
between 1915 and 1929, 'I confess that the impression
made by these reports was so strong that I am ready to
give up my opposition to the existence of thought transference. . . . I should even be prepared to lend the support
of psychoanalysis to the matter of telepathy.' Dr Jones was
unnerved by this, feeling sure that to accept telepathy
would be fatal for psychoanalysis, and he issued a circular
letter describing its dangers; the future of psychoanalysis
depended on its looking and behaving in a predictable
way; if it were to gain any place among medical treatments it
needed to drop all apparent contact with 'old wives' tales'.

But 'The mysteriousness which reigns everywhere' – to
which he referred in a love letter when young – still
summoned his curiosity in later years. It was because of
the need for diplomacy, exerted on behalf of the scientific
standing of psychoanalysis, that he chose not to give public
support to E.S.P. experiments or to investigations into

other forms of parapsychology. For instance, at the end of a paper on dreams and telepathy Freud asks, 'Have I given you the impression that I am secretly inclined to support the reality of telepathy in the occult sense? If so, I should very much regret that it is so difficult to avoid giving such an impression. In reality, however, I was anxious to be strictly impartial. I have every reason to be so, for I have no opinion; I know nothing about it.'

But because Freud, in the same paper, illustrated the neurotic and emotional tendencies in those who described telepathic experiences, it does not mean that in other cases he completely discounted the possibility of their existence. In fact elsewhere, he wrote, 'telepathy may be the original archaic method by which individuals understood each other and which has been pushed into the background by the better method of communication by means of signs apprehended by the sense organs. But such older methods may have persisted in the background and may still manifest themselves under certain conditions.'

Analysts and students of parapsychology have written some very cogent, thought-provoking papers about these 'certain conditions'; notably Servadio, Hollos, Fodor, Eisenbud and Ehrenwald. The fact that Freud himself found E.S.P. fascinating encouraged a number of analysts to take psychical research seriously. Other Freudians echo his 'I know nothing about it', but they are probably found among those who prefer to work with the better-known hazards of the unconscious, rather than to speculate about current examples of archaic methods of communication.

In May, Lord Balfour, opening the Hebrew University in Jerusalem, referred to the three men, all Jews, whom he considered to have most influenced modern thought – Bergson, Einstein and Freud. Nowadays one takes it for granted that this sort of acclaim should have come within Freud's lifetime, yet it is surprising when one looks back at the outraged manner in which his ideas were first received. The upheaval set going by the first world war was largely responsible for the change in the attitude of educated people towards Freud's findings; disapproval changed to interest, then tolerance, and finally to some sort of agreement. So much that was terrifying, devastating, and painful had taken place during those years of trench fighting, incessant bombardment and air attack, so many of the old ideas and ways of life had been shaken into new meaning and new dimensions by the political implications of the Russian Revolution, that the Freudian revolution of thought, concerning the needs and demands of instinct, appeared less shocking than before. The brute force glimpsed in the individual psychology of man could be better, or anyhow more easily, accepted in the light of the brutality of group responses and activities. It must not be forgotten, also, that for the first time civilians played an essential part in military strategy and defence. The 1914–18 war was the first of its kind to affect whole populations; moreover, communications were swifter, so that even distant battle fronts were felt to be in touch with the home governments. Thus it was that, at the very time when Freud's days seemed to be numbered, not only did his achievement begin to be universally recognized but the methods which he had devised were established and handed on.

Had these methods not enabled so many people to overcome, or at any rate adjust to, their varying neuroses; had they instead, as some critics declared, injured or misled neurotics and ruined the students of psychoanalysis, then his teaching would most certainly not have lasted. Many cults and beliefs have claimed to free people from their personal anxieties and mental troubles, and many will no doubt be evolved in the future, but psychoanalysis substantiated its claims. Psychoanalysts never make immodest claims, and are always trying to avoid being thought of as miracle workers. Especially in the early days, some of the first cures and improvements for which analysts were responsible led a number of patients and their families to expect miracles. Freud warned all and sundry against this, and his followers have never ceased to issue such warnings. Thus their technique will always contribute to psychotherapy, and to the understanding of personality and the upbringing of children.

In December 1925 Abraham died. His illness had been difficult to diagnose, but later was thought to have been cancer of the lung. During the last year he had had a difference of opinion with Freud over the production of the first film about psychoanalysis, which Freud felt would inevitably be trashy; he had no desire to advise on it or be in any way connected. Abraham felt that it would be better if an orthodox analyst were to advise on it rather than a 'wild one' (wild was the term used for analysts not trained by the recognized training institutes). This was probably the only issue over which the two men were in radical disagreement, and would most certainly have cleared up before long. Freud wrote the first short obituary notice, which contained the line from Horace *'integer vitae, scelerisque purus'* (a man of upright life and free of stain). He wrote to Jones, 'Exaggerations on the occasion of a death I have always found to be especially distasteful. I was careful to avoid them, but I feel this citation to be really truthful'. He continued, 'Who would have thought when we were all together in the Harz Mountains that he would be the first to leave this senseless life? We must work on and hold together. No one can replace the personal loss, but for the work no one must be irreplaceable. I shall soon fall out – it is to be hoped that the others will do so only much later but the work must be continued, in comparison with whose dimensions we are all equally small.'

Eitingon accepted the onerous position of President of the International Association left vacant by Abraham's death, and Anna Freud took Eitingon's place as secretary.

Freud's autobiography was completed that year as one of a series of medical autobiographies. It is valuable as a brief account of his scientific career and the development of his ideas, and dwells only slightly on his personal life. He also wrote a paper on 'The Resistances to Psycho-Analysis' for the periodical *Revue Juive*. This points out that there have always been ambivalent reactions towards anything new – the dread of it and the eager search for it – and that, since civilization depends on the control of primitive instincts, the revelations of psychoanalysis were bound to constitute a threat and might be thought likely to undermine control. Two clinical papers were published that year, one entitled 'Negation' and the other 'Some Psychological Consequences of the Anatomical Distinction between the Sexes'.

Early in 1926 Freud's heart gave cause for worry; twice, when he was out walking, he had attacks of angina pectoris which he himself attributed to an intolerance of tobacco. He underwent some treatment for this, but wrote that he could not be angry with his heart since heart trouble opened up the prospect of a 'not too delayed and not too miserable an exit'. In the same letter he wrote, 'I should deem myself a man to be envied. To grow so old, to find so much warm love in family and friends, so much expectation of success in such a venturesome undertaking, if not the success itself; who else has attained so much?'

While he was leading a semi-invalid existence he would take a morning drive out to the green suburbs before beginning work with his drastically reduced number of patients. 'Lilac time in Vienna, what a pity one has to grow old and ill before being able to discover how beautiful the spring can be.'

The prospect of his seventieth birthday tempted him to escape by spending a week in a sanatorium, but he realized this would be too cowardly and unkind to his many well-wishers. Special articles appeared in newspapers, and showers of telegrams and letters came from all over the world. He said of the commemoration essays from the Jewish B'nai B'rith Lodge, 'They were pretty harmless on the whole. I regard myself as one of the most dangerous enemies of religion but they don't seem to have any suspicion of that', and, 'Altogether the Jews are treating me like a national hero, although my service to the Jewish cause is confined to the single point that I have never disowned my Jewishness'.

Thanking his friends and pupils for the handsome donation made to him (four-fifths of which he gave to the *Verlag* and one-fifth to the Vienna clinic) he appealed to them to bear witness to the number of good friends he had, but also not to be deceived by apparent success and thus underestimate the strength of the opposition yet to be overcome. In this he was perfectly right. The opposition to psychoanalysis may take different turns and different shapes, but it is in the nature of things that an understanding of unconscious processes raises the resistance of conscious reasoning.

Freud's heart condition improved during his summer holiday, and he saw two patients daily at that time. After the holiday he took five instead of six, but raised his fees from twenty to twenty-five dollars an hour. Instead of conducting further meetings of the Vienna Society, he invited a small number of selected members to his home on every second Friday for an evening's scientific discussion.

Ferenczi, unsatisfied and isolated in Budapest, went to New York for six months to lecture at the New School of Social Research. While there, he went a long way towards upsetting every analyst by claiming to have trained eight or nine people, mostly lay analysts, whom he hoped would be recognized as a separate society by the International Association. They were not. The New York analysts had already condemned therapeutic practice by non-medical therapists, and as the months wore on Ferenczi was almost entirely ostracized.

The problem of lay analysis was in the forefront of discussion at many of the institutes. Freud himself had no wish for psychoanalysis to be thought of as the 'mere housemaid of psychiatry', and wished it to have a place in a much wider world contributing towards research in anthropology, history, education and upbringing, art, and social institutions such as marriage, law, religion and even government. He wrote *The Question of Lay Analysis* in 1926, after a very unbalanced patient had brought an action against Theodor Reik for harmful treatment, invoking the Austrian law against quackery. Reik won the case, but it was at this time that the American analysts' allegiance to medicine became rigid. Independent of other associations, they made lay analysis illegal.

Freud's book is one of the best examples of his brilliance of exposition. Cast in the form of a dialogue between himself and an interested listener, it illustrates clearly what psychoanalysis is and does, and remains the most persuasive plea for a liberal attitude towards it. The problem of whether a student should submit himself to an extensive medical training before he begins the long psychoanalytic training is still debated today. Freud wished that there could be a special training college for analysts which would teach the rudiments of anatomy, physiology, pathology, biology, embryology and evolution, mythology, the psychology of religion and the classics of literature. He also wished his lay analysts to arrange for a doctor to be the first consultant for any patient, thus showing that he believed in the possibility of easy cooperation between analysts and medicine. Many of the early analysts in England whose names are remembered gratefully were non-medical. They include Ella Sharpe, J. C. Flugel, Joan Riviere, Barbara Low, James and Alix Strachey and Melanie Klein.

Cooperation between analysis and medicine has now been obtained, though by no means all doctors are willing to send patients for analytic treatment. For years a feud smouldered between American and European analysts concerning this vexed question – a feud which only abated after the last war; the problem still remains unsolved. Freud never realized that in other countries the profession of doctor is not held in as high esteem as it is in Austria, and he remained unsympathetic to the American view. He did not take into account the fact that professional medical men in the United States had only recently become distinguished from unqualified practitioners. As in most issues, he took the long view; and there is no doubt that, as the concepts of psychoanalysis become better known and more trusted, non-medical people will be welcomed as trainees in analysis, and will be accepted as specialists after five or six years of study. In the 1920s Ernest Jones in England and Brill in America felt the time unsuitable for anything but a close relationship with the medical profession, and that the whole status of psychoanalysis as a science depended on such a relationship. Ferenczi, with his swift training of lay analysts, could therefore only be regarded by these two (as well as by many others) as a threat.

After the Innsbruck Congress in 1927 the Committee, reduced to vanishing point by internal disagreements and by Abraham's death, was converted into a group of officials of the International Association. Among the difficulties they had to cope with were the financial commitments and debts of the *Verlag*, which Freud was very averse to selling to a commercial firm. A generous donation from a private benefactor enabled it to carry on for the time being, but two years later there was another crisis. On this occasion it was rescued from bankruptcy by donations from the Budapest Society, Marie Bonaparte, Ruth Brunswick, Brill and an anonymous American patient.

In 1927 Freud added a supplement to his essay on Michelangelo's *Moses*, and wrote papers on fetishism and humour, and an important little book called *The Future of an Illusion*, which he described, soon after he had written it, as childish, but which gave rise to many acrimonious controversies about the basis for religious thought and behaviour.

Ernest Jones felt that Freud's most valuable post-war clinical contribution was *Inhibitions – Symptoms and Anxiety*, which was published in 1926. It is thought that Freud wrote it to try and clarify his own ideas, but it remains an essential book for serious students, and makes a great contribution to the understanding of mental disturbances. In it Freud goes back to one of his earliest conceptions, that of *defence*, which he had for so long replaced with repression; he now regarded the latter as only *one* of the means of defence which the ego uses to keep itself free from the tensions of fear and conflict. Repression in hysteria is contrasted with reaction formation (thinking or doing the opposite), isolation, and 'undoing' (a form of reparation or restitution) found in obsessional neurosis. Freud admitted that he had been wrong to think of morbid anxiety as transformed libido, and agreed with Jones's view (though he did not quote him) that the anxiety comes from the ego itself. He goes on to discriminate between 'real anxiety', which concerns something objective, and morbid anxiety, the cause of which is unknown; it may emanate from dread of *id* [1]impulses, and may attach itself to substitute objects as in neurotic phobias. Freud maintained that this kind of anxiety in males was inevitably attended by a fear of castration, and in females by a fear of not being loved. He goes on to describe the concomitant helplessness felt during traumatic experiences, and distinguishes between id anxiety, which he counted as instinc-

[1] See page 130

tual and involuntary (such as may take place at birth), and ego anxiety, which takes place rather on the lines of an inoculation in order to avoid the actual catastrophe by which, for some neurotic reason, the patient feels threatened.

He points out how important the mastering of anxiety is for children, reminding readers of the relief afforded to the small child playing at 'come back' games or throwing things down to be picked up. (Later analysts worked this idea out in detail, seeing much of adult life as ways of easing anxious tension.) Freud, realizing that the prolonged infancy of man makes him prone to neurosis, analyses those infantile experiences which may constitute a situation so dangerous that the response is retained in full strength in the unconscious, requiring thenceforth thorough repression or an intricate defence. The factor of quantity – numbers of frightening experiences, degree of deprivation, instances of adult severity – is held to be responsible for many cases of pathological fear.

In 1929 Ernst Freud persuaded his father to consult another famous oral surgeon, Professor Schroeder of Berlin. The new prosthesis made there, though by no means perfect, was an improvement on the old one. Freud was attended by a Viennese doctor, who prescribed for him the use of orthoform, one of the novacain group; so that Freud became a beneficiary of his own early work. Later this was found to set up a pre-cancerous condition, and had to be stopped.

About this time Marie Bonaparte persuaded Freud to engage Dr Max Schur to watch over his general health daily and to remain in constant contact with his surgeons. Schur had been analytically trained. At their first interview Freud laid down the basic rule that Schur should never keep the truth from him, however painful, and Schur at once saw how sincere a request this was. Shaking hands on it Freud said, 'I can stand a great deal of pain and I hate sedatives, but I trust you will not let me suffer unnecessarily'. Except for a few weeks in 1939, Schur was close to Freud throughout the last ten years of his life; his consideration and resourcefulness were unsurpassable. He and Anna made ideal guardians, alleviating the ceaseless discomforts and evaluating the slightest change in the local condition. Their care and skill undoubtedly prolonged Freud's life. Freud was a model patient, touchingly grateful and completely uncomplaining. A favourite expression of his was, 'It's no use quarrelling with fate'.

Physical pain must have made writing nearly impossible but in 1929 the most brilliant of his contributions to the psychology of literature was completed in an introductory essay to a new edition of Dostoyevsky's *The Brothers Karamazov*. Freud felt that the episode with the Grand Inquisitor was one of the highest achievements of the world's literature, but was considerably disappointed in Dostoyevsky as a man – someone who looked as though he were destined to lead mankind to better things, but ended up as a 'docile reactionary'. He pointed out that the three great masterpieces of all time had to do with patricide: Sophocles' *Oedipus Rex*, Shakespeare's *Hamlet* and *The Brothers Karamazov*. To Theodor Reik, who wrote a review of this essay, Freud said, 'You are right in supposing I don't really like Dostoyevsky ... That is because my patience with pathological nature is drained away in actual analyses. In art and in life I am intolerant of them. That is a personal characteristic of my own which needn't hold good with other people.'

In this same year Ernest Jones and Edward Glover were able to tell Freud of the success of the report on psychoanalysis made by the British Medical Association. This firmly established psychoanalysis in England, but made Ferenczi increasingly bitter and hostile both to Brill and to Jones. An overt split over lay analysis was avoided at the Oxford conference that year, but Ferenczi's divergence from orthodox procedure was further made clear in the paper which he read on the inadvisability of paying much attention to childhood fantasies, stating that definite traumas, especially the unkindness of parents, lay at the root of neuroses. The year 1930 saw Freud and Ferenczi coming to better terms as a result of a long and frank discussion, though Ferenczi still remained acutely sensitive to the slights which he felt he had sustained.

10 The last years in Vienna

Civilization and Its Discontents was published in 1930. In this book Freud gave an account of his views for the consumption of sociologists. 'Sociology', he said elsewhere, 'can be nothing other than applied psychology.' The feeling described by Romain Rolland of being mystically identified with the universe Freud called an oceanic feeling. He could not bring himself to believe this to be a primary constituent of the mind, and traced it to earliest infancy when no distinction is made between the self and the outer world.

Freud regarded speculations about the purpose of life as pointless. The aim behind human behaviour seemed to him to be no more and no less than the search for happiness – not just happiness in a narrow sense, but the search for bliss and peace of mind. In the more intense form he saw the pleasure-pain principle as only a temporary episode, continuation of pleasure being experienced merely as contentedness. Freud thought that human happiness had little to do with any purpose of the universe, and that the chances of unhappiness seemed to lie far more readily to hand. The sources of these he listed under the headings of bodily suffering, dangers from the outer world and disturbance in relations with fellow men. He counted the last as perhaps the most painful of all.

Freud wrote that civilization came about through the discovery that if a number of men placed limits on their own gratifications they became stronger than any single, uninhibited man. The strength of this united body would then be counted as 'right' against any single individual, whose strength would be condemned as 'brute force'. Freud saw the first requisite of any culture to be justice – the assurance that a law, once made, will not be broken in favour of any individual. Hence the never-ending conflict between the claims of the individual for personal gratification and the demands of society which so often oppose them. Listing the restrictions placed on one of the instinctive drives, the prohibitions on auto-erotism, incest, perversions, homosexuality and promiscuity, Freud pointed out that these restrictions gave the impression of a function severely disabled, if not slowly atrophying, and described the result as reducing energy and often ending in neurosis.

Considering the precept 'Thou shalt love thy neighbour as thyself', Freud wrote that this high demand comes about as a reaction formation to counter the strength of the aggressive instinct. 'Culture has to call up every possible reinforcement to erect barriers against aggression, which is the most powerful obstacle to culture.'

Man's characteristic way of dealing with aggression, according to Freud, was to *internalize* it in the part of the self called the super-ego or conscience which then exercised against the ego the harshness it would have liked to expend on other objects. This tension between ego and super-ego constitutes what is known as the sense of guilt. Freud considered that this powerful emotion arises not from any inborn sense of sin but from the fear of losing love. The sense of guilt is the specific response to repressed aggressiveness, and since it is so largely unconscious, its manifestation is the feeling of uneasiness, general discontent and unhappiness. The book can be summed up in Freud's own words: 'The price of progress in civilization is paid for by forfeiting happiness through the heightening of the sense of guilt'. Only mildly optimistic about the future of society, Freud hoped that, 'In the course of time changes will be carried out in our civilization so that it becomes more satisfying to our needs. Also we may accustom ourselves to the idea that there are certain difficulties *inherent in the very nature of culture which will not yield to any efforts at reform.*'

Freud's heart and abdominal conditions required treatment at the cottage sanatorium where he had been several times before, and he improved his health through once more cutting down his smoking. While in Berlin to procure yet another prosthesis, he wrote in collaboration with W. C. Bullitt, the American Ambassador, a psychoanalytic study of President Wilson (though it was not published till 1967). It was to Bullitt that Freud showed how hopeful he was that the Germans would be able to contain the Nazi movement: 'A nation that produced Goethe could not possibly go to the bad'. Very shortly afterwards he had to revise this judgement.

He was awarded the Goethe prize, and Anna Freud read his address for him in Frankfurt. Ernest Jones hoped that this would lead to a Nobel prize, but Freud's awareness of the opposition to psychoanalysis was more realistic. That same year Freud's mother died at the age of ninety-five. He wrote of his feeling of release: 'I was not allowed to die as long as she was alive, and now I may. Somehow the values of life have notably changed in the deeper layers.'

During this period one of Freud's training analysands, Eve Rosenfeld, was inadvertently made privy to the fact that Freud's symptoms were serious. This upset her, but she tried not to mention it during her next session. Sensing her hesitation, Freud prompted her to reveal what lay behind it, giving her her most significant 'lesson' in analytic technique by saying, 'We have only one aim and one loyalty, to psychoanalysis – if you break this rule [the rule for the patient to say whatever comes into his or her head] you injure something much more important than any consideration you owe me'.

In October Freud underwent another operation and skin was taken from his arm, as was done several times, to graft on to the exposed part of the jaw. After this he went down with broncho-pneumonia for ten days, but was back at work with four patients in November, and by the end of the year was in much better health. In 1931 he had to decline an invitation, which he had been delighted to receive, to deliver the annual Huxley lecture at London University. No German had been invited to give this since Virchow in 1898, and Freud was a great admirer of T. H. Huxley.

His seventy-fifth birthday cast its shadow upon him early. Unwillingly he had agreed that a fund should be collected for the *Verlag*, which, as ever, needed money, but he wrote realistically of the wealth of emotions precipitated by the offer. 'Feeble old people are often overcome by these [emotions] and a little later succumb to the after-effects. You get nothing for nothing, and you have to pay heavily for living too long.'

In April 1931 another operation took place, and this made any kind of celebration impossible. A fund of 50,000 marks (£2500) had been collected, so Freud had a cheque for 20,000 marks with which to repay the loans for the *Verlag*. There was a banquet in New York, a mass of letters and telegrams (one from Einstein, of whom Freud had said when they had had an enjoyable first encounter, 'He knows as much psychoanalysis as I know physics'), and 'a forest of flowers'. Thanking Marie Bonaparte for the Grecian vase she had sent, Freud added, 'It is a pity one cannot take it into one's grave' – a wish that was strangely fulfilled, since his ashes now repose in that vase.

The general economic crisis of 1931 – so disastrous in its political consequences – pressed on everyone's life. Analysts were feeling the pinch in their practices, and in July they decided to postpone the Congress another year.

The prosthesis was so uncomfortable that a great deal of money was spent on fetching a famous American Professor of dental and oral surgery from Berlin, in the hope that he would be able to alleviate the distress, but the result was unsuccessful. Freud, on hearing details about the day of rejoicing in his birthplace, Freiberg (now Puibor), where, to mark the occasion of his birthday, a bronze plaque had been placed on the house where he was born, wrote, 'Since the Goethe prize last year, the world has changed its treatment of me into an unwilling recognition, but only to show me how little that really matters. What a contrast a bearable prosthesis would be, one that didn't clamour to be the main object of one's existence.'

In October Ferenczi spent two days in Vienna to discuss with Freud their differences in analytical method. Ferenczi deemed it a necessary part of analytic technique to replace parental severity, even going so far as to allow patients to kiss him and to analyse him if they felt like it. In Freud's view, however, the loss of objectivity, the absence of analytic 'working through' of the dread of the father, reduced the analytic situation to a playful game, and in an important letter to Ferenczi he makes this view clear and comprehensible. 'What one does in one's technique one has to defend openly. I too am aware that in the time of the Nibelungs a kiss was a harmless greeting granted to every guest. I am further of opinion that analysis is possible even in Soviet Russia, where, so far as the State is concerned, there is full sexual freedom [this was true then]. But that does not alter the facts that we are not living in Russia, and that with us a kiss signifies a certain erotic intimacy. We have held to the conclusion that patients are to be refused erotic gratifications. You know too that where more extensive gratifications (coitus) are not to be had, milder caresses very easily take over their role – in love affairs on the stage, for instance.'

Freud went on to point out that Ferenczi would be followed by more extreme analysts, who would think, 'Why stop at a kiss? Certainly one gets further when one adopts 'pawing' as well, which after all doesn't make a baby.' He went on, 'Soon we shall have accepted in the technique of analysis the whole repertoire of *demi-viergerie* and petting parties, resulting in an enormous increase of interest in psychoanalysis. The new adherent may claim too much of this interest for himself, and the younger colleagues find it hard to stop at the point they originally intended. God the Father Ferenczi gazing at the lively scene thus created will perhaps say to himself: maybe after all I should have halted in my technique of motherly affection before the kiss . . . In this warning I do not think I have said anything you do not know yourself, but since you like playing a tender mother role with others, perhaps you do so also with yourself, and so compel me to make a brutal fatherly admonition and thus to be quite blunt.' He finished, 'I do not expect to make any impression on you – the necessary basis for that is absent in our relations. The need for definite independence seems to me to be stronger in you than you recognize. At least I have done what I could in my father role.'

That October Freud published two papers in the *Zeitschrift*. One was on libidinal types (the erotic, the obsessive and the narcissistic, and three composite forms of them), and was an important addition to the subject of characterology. The other was on female sexuality, a theme which Freud always confessed to finding difficult, with only a couple of outstanding conclusions of which he felt sure.

The last and worst financial crisis of the *Verlag* was

solved when Freud decided that it could not be run personally, and issued an appeal to the International Association to take responsibility for it. The various Societies responded at once (the British, for instance, subscribed £500 in the first week, and the Wiesbaden Congress laid an obligation on all members to subscribe 36 dollars a year). Martin Freud took over the management of the *Verlag*, and Jones became President of the International Association for the second time, replacing Eitingon who had had a slight stroke.

Freud's birthday that year passed as he always wished – just like any other day. 'In the morning a visit to Kagram with the dogs [he had recently begun to like owning dogs]. In the afternoon the usual visit to Pichler [for attention to his mouth]. Then four hours' analytic work, and a game of cards in the evening. Some doubts whether one should be glad to have lived to this date, and then resignation.' He wrote of the lack of fresh applications to him for treatment either from patients or trainees. 'They are of course quite right; I am too old, and working with me is too precarious. It is pleasant enough to think my "supply" has lasted longer than the "demand".'

Ferenczi's withdrawal had become more pronounced, and writing to Marie Bonaparte about his satisfaction at the success of the Wiesbaden Congress Freud said, 'Ferenczi is a bitter drop in the cup. His wise wife has told me I should think of him as a sick child! You are right: psychic and intellectual decay is far worse than the unavoidable bodily one.'

It had been a bad year, with five operations and a severe attack of 'flu in November. However, in March, when the *Verlag* affairs had been so desperate, he had offered to help it by writing a new series of introductory lectures illustrating the progress that had taken place in his ideas in the fifteen years since the first series appeared. 'Certainly this work comes more from a need of the *Verlag* than any need on my part, but one should always be doing something in which one might be interrupted – better than going down in a state of laziness.'

One must admire his endurance and courage. Not many people achieved such a philosophy surrounded by the depression of the outer world at that time even when they were not ravaged by personal discomfort and ageing; 1933 saw Hitler's persecutions in force. Many analysts had already emigrated from Europe. Freud wrote to Marie Bonaparte in Paris, 'People fear that the nationalistic extravagance in Germany may extend to our little country. I have been advised to flee to Switzerland or France. That is nonsense. I don't believe there is any danger here. If they kill me – good. It is one kind of death like another. But probably this is only cheap boasting.'

He wrote in the same sort of vein to Ferenczi, for whom, despite their theoretical differences, he remained concerned and considerate. Ferenczi was very ill, the anaemia from which he was suffering having attacked the spinal cord and brain, and augmented his psychotic trends. Paranoic outbursts followed, and he died suddenly on 24 May. Freud wrote to Jones, 'Ferenczi takes with him a part of the old time; then with my departure another [era] will begin which you will see. Fate. Resignation. That is all.'

Replying to Dr Roy Winn of Sydney, who proposed that he should write a further, more intimate autobiography, he said, 'Even the amount of autobiography (exhibitionism) needed for writing *The Interpretation of Dreams* I found trying enough. Personally I ask nothing more from the world than that it should leave me in peace and devote its interest to psychoanalysis instead.'

It is quite clear that his pleasure and involvement in the young and in the living never forsook him for long. In a letter to Jones he said, 'In all the familiar uncertainty of life one may envy parents the joy and hopes which soon centre round the new human creature; whereas with old people one must be glad when the scales are nearly balanced between the inevitable need of final rest and the wish to enjoy a while longer the love and friendship of those near. I believe I have discovered that the longing for ultimate rest is not something ordinary, elementary and primary, but an expression of the need to be rid of the feeling of inadequacy which affects age – especially in the smallest details of life.' Reading this important sentence from an important letter one wonders whether, if Freud could have returned to the prime of life armed with the experience of old age, he might have written something of enormous significance to do with the sense of inadequacy being always bound up with the sense of guilt at the inability to repair. Perhaps he would have attributed ageing (especially premature ageing) and death itself to this sort of guilt rather than to a 'death instinct'.

Freud continued to think that, though Nazism would inevitably extend to Austria, 'special laws against Jews are out of the question because of the clauses in our peace treaty which expressly guarantee the rights of minorities'. He believed that the League of Nations would at once take action if Hitler violated these rights and that, 'France and her old allies would never allow Austria to join Germany'. But soon after writing these hopeful remarks he wrote to Marie Bonaparte, 'The world is turning into an enormous prison. Germany is the worst cell. What will happen in the Austrian cell is quite uncertain.' Of the Nazis he wrote, 'They began with Bolshevism as their deadly enemy and they will end with something indistinguishable from it – except that Bolshevism, after all, adopted revolutionary ideals, whereas those of Hitlerism are mediaeval and reactionary.' When a bonfire was made of his books in Berlin in May 1933, Freud was unperturbed. His comment was, 'What progress we are making! In the Middle Ages they would have burnt me, nowadays they are content with burning my books!' He was not to know that, had he continued to live in Austria, his body too would have been burnt in a concentration camp.

By the end of 1933 Ernest Jones was the only remaining member in Europe of the original Committee. Abraham and Ferenczi were dead, Rank had left the analysts, Sachs was in Boston and Eitingon had just left for Palestine, where he had that year organized a Psycho-Analytical Society; it still flourishes.

1934 saw the flight of the remaining Jewish analysts from Germany and the liquidation of psychoanalysts in that country. Astonishingly, the Nazis were able to obliterate almost all knowledge of Freud and his work, so that even by the 1950s less was known about him in Germany than, for example, in either Brazil or Japan. In June 1933 the German Society for Psychotherapy had come under Nazi control. Kretschmer, the President, promptly resigned, and his position was as promptly taken on by C. G. Jung, who became editor of the *Zentralblatt für Psychotherapie*. In 1936 he was joined by Göring as co-editor, and he did not resign till 1940. His chief function was to act as discriminator between Aryan and Jewish psychology, emphasizing the value of the former. A Swiss psychiatrist at once protested against this violation of the neutrality of science, and Jung, then and later, was greatly criticized for his action. In 1936 the German Society was forced to withdraw from membership of the International Psycho-Analytical Association. It was forbidden to give training analyses, and no psychoanalytic terms were allowed in lectures.

In March that year the Gestapo seized all the property of the *Verlag*, though, thanks to Martin Freud's energy, it continued to function till the Nazis confiscated it in 1938.

Radium treatment spared Freud for a year from any operation. Then Dr Ludwig Schloss, who had been trained at the Curie Institute, discovered that the metal in the prosthesis produced a secondary radiation, so another apparatus was built to obviate this. From Grinzing, a lovely hillside garden suburb of Vienna, Freud wrote to Arnold Zweig about a play which the latter had written about Napoleon. 'So you have just dashed off a new piece from the life of that terrible scamp Napoleon who, fixated as he was on his puberty fantasies, favoured by incredible luck and uninhibited by any bonds except to his family, roved through the world like a somnambulist only to founder at the end in megalomania. There has hardly ever been such a genius to whom every trace of nobility was so alien – such a classical anti-gentleman.'

From 1935 onwards Freud's interest in the dual subjects of Moses and Monotheism engrossed him. He felt that he could not publish the results, for his ideas culminated in the formula 'that religion owes its strength not to any real literal truth but to a historical truth'. Since it was, he believed, the Catholic Church in Austria which protected analysts from Nazism, and since such a point of view would certainly antagonize the Catholic authorities, to publish his book would jeopardize both his Viennese colleagues and psycho-analysis as a whole. Also, he suspected that the historical basis of the Moses story was not solid enough. 'So I remain silent. It is enough that I myself can believe in the solution of the problem. It has pursued me through my whole life.'

Since talking was such a problem for Freud, the letters which he wrote in these last years must be treasured as examples of his daily wisdom, kindness and interest. In Ernest Jones's long biography, the whole of a letter which he wrote to an unknown mother in America is quoted. There is only room here for a few sentences: 'Dear Mrs.. .. I gather from your letter that your son is a homosexual. May I question you why you avoid using the term? Homosexuality is assuredly no advantage, but it is nothing to be ashamed of, no vice, no degradation. It cannot be classified as an illness; we consider it to be a variation of the sexual function, produced by a certain arrest of sexual development. Many highly respectable individuals of ancient and modern times have been homosexuals (Plato, Michelangelo, Leonardo da Vinci, etc.). It is a great injustice to persecute homosexuality as a crime, and cruel too.'

Freud went on to say that analysts cannot promise to replace homosexuality with heterosexuality, though in a certain number of cases, 'We succeed in developing the blighted germs of heterosexual tendencies which are present in every homosexual. It is a question of the quality and the age of the individual. The result of treatment cannot be predicted.' But, 'What analysis can do for your son runs in a different line. If he is unhappy, neurotic, torn by conflicts, inhibited in his social life, analysis may bring him peace of mind, and full efficiency, whether he remains a homosexual or gets changed.'

He wrote of his birthday that year that seventy-nine was 'a quite irrational number'. It had been a miserable time for him personally, with operations in March and April, and on the day itself neither he nor Schur nor Anna could get the 'monster' into his mouth. Pichler had to be called in to do so. He continued to read all he could of Jewish history, and wondered if a certain Prince Thotmes, mentioned in connexion with excavations in Tel-el-Amarna, was 'his Moses'. He wished he had money to further the research there.

Jokingly, he asked Jones if he could put HFRSM after his name when in May he was made an Honorary Fellow of the Royal Society of Medicine in London. In June he wrote an open letter commemorating Thomas Mann's sixtieth birthday. Among the prospects awaiting him on his eightieth birthday were articles in the Press all over the world. He wrote of these to Arnold Zweig, 'What nonsense to think of making good at such a questionable date the ill-treatment of a long life. No, rather let us stay enemies.' This birthday passed off quietly, but it took him more than six weeks to cope with all the congratulations he had to answer. Einstein wrote to him telling of his recent experience of having Freud's theory of repression proved to him, which caused Freud much pleasure, as did a visit from Thomas Mann, and the presentation of an Address signed by Thomas Mann, Romain Rolland, Jules Romain, H. G. Wells, Virginia Woolf, Stefan Zweig and 191 other writers and artists.

Of course there were many personal callers. One asked Freud how he felt, and got the answer, 'How a man of eighty feels is not a topic for conversation'. The highest recognition he ever received, and the one he most treasured, was the Corresponding Membership of the Royal Society. No university, however, bestowed an honorary degree on Freud, the only one he ever received being from Clark University, thirty years before.

In July he had to have two very painful operations, and for the first time since 1923 unmistakable cancer was found. The doctors had for the last five years warded it off by their continuous removal of pre-cancerous tissue. The Conference that year took place at Marienbad, so that Anna Freud should not be far off from Freud in case she was needed.

In January 1937 Freud lost his female chow, Jofi, which saddened him greatly. Only a month before he had written to Marie Bonaparte that a love of animals meant, 'Affection without any ambivalence, the simplicity of life free from the conflicts of civilization. And in spite of the remoteness in the organic development, there is nevertheless a feeling of close relationship, of undeniably belonging together.' It was during this winter that Marie Bonaparte let him know that she had acquired his letters to Fliess. He wrote that he would have had to buy them himself, 'If the seller had come to me directly' and, 'Our correspondence was the most intimate you could imagine; it would be most distressing had they fallen into strange hands'.

In a letter to Stefan Zweig he wrote of the sorry state of the world, and then listed the remaining consolations: 'The feeling of belonging together with a few others in the certainty that the same things remain precious, the same values incontestable', then of his work, 'No one can predict how later epochs will assess it. I myself am not so sure; doubt can never be divorced from research and I have assuredly not dug up more than a fragment of the truth.'

11 Freedom in London – death

The Nazis invaded Austria in 1938. Despite Freud's known determination to stay in Vienna whatever happened, Jones decided to make a final effort to travel to Vienna to change Freud's mind. At this point, we should take note of the ceaseless contributions which Ernest Jones made to Freud, his teacher and friend, to psychoanalysis, and to the reputation which, because of his work, England now has in this field. Differing from Freud only on the questions of lay analysis, the therapeutic methods used by Melanie Klein in children's analyses, and the mental stability, or rather instability, of Rank and Ferenczi, he initiated the practice of psychoanalysis in London, and trained and taught many of the first brilliant members of the London Institute. It was he who convinced other English doctors of the importance of Freud's methods, and he never ceased working to enlarge and enrich the publication of psychoanalytic research.

He was not only a clever, tactful administrator; his writings and therapeutic successes bear testimony to his understanding and subtlety as an analyst. Psychologists in Europe particularly should never forget the perseverance and patience which he showed on behalf of Freud and of psychoanalysis in those early days, when the insecurity of their position and the novelty of their ideas often caused his colleagues to be unrealistically depressed or elated. Jones was a modest man, so it needs perspicacity to realize what a debt English psychoanalysis owes him. Freud wrote to him in 1938, 'I am sometimes perturbed by the idea that you think we believe you are simply wishing to do your duty without appreciating the deep and sincere feelings expressed in your actions. I assure you this is not so – we recognize your friendliness, count on it and fully reciprocate it. This is a solitary expression of my feelings, for between beloved friends much should be obvious and remain unexpressed.'

In March 1938 Jones took a plane to Prague (there was no direct flight to Vienna at that time), and completed the journey by monoplane. At the *Verlag* premises youths, armed with knives and pistols, were holding Martin Freud under arrest. These 'Nazi authorities' were counting the petty cash. Jones was put under arrest too for an hour or so, despite his many connexions with the British Embassy.

When Freud's house was similarly invaded, the Nazis were considerably disconcerted by Martha's actions. She behaved, as people do in an emergency, in complete accord with her innermost nature. She invited the intruders to be seated, and in her most hospitable manner placed the household money on the table, saying, as at dinner time, 'Won't the gentlemen help themselves?'. Anna Freud then escorted them to the safe. The loot amounted to approximately 6,000 Austrian schillings (£300). They were debating about this when a gaunt figure appeared in the doorway. Freud could frown with blazing eyes in a positively Old Testament manner; observing him the Nazis said they would come another time and hastily withdrew! A week later the Gestapo searched the apartment seeking for anti-Nazi documents. Even then they did not enter Freud's own rooms.

Anna Freud was detained by them for a whole day – the blackest in Freud's life. He spent it pacing up and down smoking an endless chain of cigars to try and deaden the mental torture of thinking what might be happening to her. Yet in his diary for that day there are only three words, *'Anna bei Gestapo'*. The silent understanding and sympathy between him and Anna must have been something very rare, the daughter's devotion being as absolute as the father's appreciation of it.

Jones had to overcome great reluctance on Freud's part before he was persuaded to leave. To the plea that he was not alone in the world, that his life was dear to many, Freud replied gently, 'Ah, if I were only alone I should long ago have done with life'. He argued that he was too weak to travel, but Jones would not accept this. Freud then fell back on the truth that no country was hospitable to immigrants in those days, owing to the general fear of unemployment. At this Jones asked for permission to return to England and try to get an exception made in his case. Freud felt that to leave his native land would be like a soldier deserting. Jones responded cleverly with the analogy of Lightoller, the second officer of the *Titanic*, who never left his ship but whom his ship left. This it was that won Freud's final acceptance.

After an interview with Sir Samuel Hoare, Jones did not find it hard to get permission for Freud and his family to live in England. But how to get the Nazis to release him? In his biography of Freud Jones remarks that great men have more friends, even in high places, than they know of. W. C. Bullitt, who was by now American Ambassador in Paris, was a personal friend of Roosevelt. Thus the President of the United States, through his Secretary of State instructed the American Chargé d'Affaires in Vienna to intervene. In Paris Bullitt let the German Ambassador to France know that a world scandal would ensue if the Nazis ill-treated Freud. Mussolini is said to have made similar representations to Hitler. Eventually the Nazis felt they did not dare risk refusing Freud an exit permit.

The Vienna Psycho-Analytical Society had concurrently decided that all their members should flee the country if possible, and that the seat of the Society should be wherever Freud settled.

Three months of anxious waiting ensued before Freud was allowed to leave. A fervent anti-Semite had been appointed to supervise the arrangements, including the financial ones, attendant on Freud's departure, but as luck would have it this man had studied chemistry under Professor Herzig, a life-long Jewish friend of Freud's, and had conceived a great respect for him which he said he now wished to extend to Freud. So he suppressed the fact that Freud had money abroad, and allowed many of the household belongings and all the antiques to be sent out of the country. Anna and Marie Bonaparte went through Freud's papers and correspondence, burning a great deal which they considered not worth taking to London. The Nazis demanded payment on all sorts of trumped-up taxes – income tax, fugitives tax, and so on – and since it was difficult for Freud to find the money Marie Bonaparte advanced Austrian schillings for this purpose. Martin

Freud was frequently called to Gestapo headquarters for questioning. The American Chargé d'Affaires, Mr Wiley, who had intervened when Anna was arrested, kept a watchful eye on the various raids and confiscations.

Freud wrote to his son Ernst in London, 'In these dark days, there are two prospects to cheer us – to rejoin you all and to die in freedom'. In the same letter, 'How far we old people will succeed in coping with the difficulties of the new home remains to be seen. You will help us in that. Nothing counts compared with the deliverance. Anna will assuredly find it easy and that is decisive, the whole undertaking would have no sense for the three of us between seventy-three and eighty-two.' (Minna still lived with them.)

Freud retained his ironic attitude towards all the formalities which had to be gone through. One of them was that he should sign a document which ran, 'I, Prof. Freud, hereby confirm that after the *Anschluss* of Austria to the German Reich I have been treated by the German authorities and particularly by the Gestapo with all the respect and consideration due to my scientific reputation; that I could live and work in full freedom, that I could continue to pursue my activities in every way I desired, that I found full support from all concerned in this respect and that I have not the slightest reason for any complaint.'

Freud had no compunction in signing this nonsense, but asked if he might add on a line. This was granted and he wrote, 'I can heartily recommend the Gestapo to anyone!'

His thoughtfulness for others never deserted him. One of his last gestures was to get Brill to issue the necessary American affidavits for Breuer's daughter-in-law and family so that they could emigrate. On 4 June Freud, with his wife and Anna and two maidservants, left the city where he had dwelt for seventy-nine years. Minna and Martin, with his family, had already left.

They spent twelve wonderful hours in Marie Bonaparte's beautiful house in Paris. She was able to tell him that his gold was safe. (The miserable experiences of the post-war inflation had taught Freud to preserve an amount of gold money as a guard against future disaster.) Marie Bonaparte could not safely take it out of Austria, so she had arranged with the Greek Embassy in Vienna to despatch it by courier to the King of Greece, who later transferred it to the Greek Embassy in London.

Ernst accompanied them on the last part of the journey. There must have been a moving scene at the reunion at Victoria Station between the Freud parents and their oldest children, Mathilde and Martin. Jones and his wife were waiting for them, and they made a quick get-away in their car. Freud, who had for weeks been learning up London with maps and guides, eagerly pointed out the landmarks to his wife.

They went first to a house which Ernst had rented for them in Elsworthy Road. Freud was enormously cheered by the garden, Primrose Hill, and the distant view of the city from this temporary home, and threw up his arms on his first stroll, remarking to Jones, 'I am almost tempted to cry out Heil Hitler!'

He was delighted by many things – the greetings from the English analysts, scientists and Jewish societies, the enthusiasm in the newspapers, and an invitation from Cleveland (USA) signed by 'the citizens of all faiths and all professions'. The medical journals published short leading articles expressing welcome. The *Lancet* wrote, 'His teachings have in their time aroused controversy more acute and antagonism more bitter than any since the days of Darwin. Now in his old age there are few psychologists of any school who do not admit their debt to him. Some of the conceptions he formulated clearly for the first time have crept into current philosophy against the stream of wilful incredulity which he himself recognized as man's natural reaction to unbearable truth.' The *British Medical Journal* said, 'The medical profession of Great Britain will feel proud that their country has offered asylum to Professor Freud and that he has chosen it as his new home.'

He was especially pleased by letters from complete strangers merely writing to say how happy they were that he had come to England. Taxi drivers knew where he lived, and the bank manager greeted him with the remark, 'I know all about you'. There were even gifts of valuable antiques from people who evidently shared Freud's pessimistic view about the chances of his collection arriving from Vienna. But of course the happiness was not entirely unalloyed. He wrote to Eitingon, 'The feeling of triumph at being freed is strongly mingled with grief, since I always loved the prison from which I have been released'. This was the only time he admitted to this love, although there are many allusions to his intense dislike of Vienna, but of course this hidden attraction must partially explain his persistent refusal to leave the city.

He hoped that the money which he and his brother Alexander had left with their four sisters (about £8000) would keep them safe in Vienna. The more violent persecution of the Jews had not yet begun, which meant that Freud was spared serious worry about them. Marie Bonaparte failed to get permission to bring them into France and fortunately Freud never knew their subsequent fate – incineration in 1944.

Until 20 Maresfield Gardens was ready (the family moved there in September) Freud spent some days at the Esplanade Hotel in Warrington Crescent. Diathermy had to be prescribed for a new suspicious spot near the scar, but for a while he felt better and treated a few patients. Nevertheless, an operation had to take place, and Pichler was fetched from Vienna. Freud felt this was the most radical operation he had had since 1923, and he never fully recovered. He was, though, able to feel at home as soon as he could join his wife in Maresfield Gardens. He said that it was a really beautiful house, though 'too good for someone who would not tenant it for long'. He spent as much time as possible in the secluded garden which led out from his consulting room at the back, filled with his loved possessions. All his furniture, books and antiques arrived six weeks after him.

Among some of his famous callers that autumn may be mentioned H. G. Wells, Professor Malinowski and Chaim Weizmann. In June came three secretaries of the Royal Society, Sir Albert Seward, Professor A. V. Hill and Mr Griffith Davies, who brought the official Charter Book of the Society for him to sign. Freud enjoyed this meeting, and was presented with a copy of the great book which contains, among others, the signatures of Isaac Newton and Charles Darwin. Salvador Dali made a quick sketch of him in July, maintaining that surrealistically Freud's cranium was reminiscent of a snail!

On 1 August the last Psycho-Analytical Congress to be held for some years took place in Paris. A sharp difference of opinion arose over the question of lay analysis, and two committees, one of European and one of American analysts, were formed to try to find a solution. The European Committee met in Freud's presence at his house in December to hear him state once more his well-known views on the subject. As it happened, the whole programme was shelved because of the war, and since then the relations between the analysts in the two continents have been harmonious.

Freud wrote to the London Yiddish Scientific Institute (he had been honorary president of the Vienna branch since 1919), 'I was very glad to get your greeting. You no doubt know that I gladly and proudly acknowledge my Jewishness, though my attitude towards any religion, including ours, is critically negative.' In August of the following year he was invited to replace their president, who had died, but he replied, 'Because of the active opposition which my book *Moses and Monotheism* evoked in Jewish circles, I doubt whether it would be in your interests to bring my name before the public eye in such a capacity. I leave the decision to you.'

By the end of 1938 he was well enough to conduct four analyses daily, and he continued to do so, with a few interruptions, until near the end of his life. That November it was for a time as warm as summer. Seated in his garden, Freud was delighted – 'It's just like May'.

He managed to add the finishing touches to the third part of *Moses* before an operation in September, but he never completed *An Outline of Psycho-Analysis*. He had begun it to fill in spare time, for he thought that Jones's book *Psycho-Analysis*, published in 1928, was quite sufficient. He kept saying he felt ashamed at writing nothing but repetitions without any new ideas. Published the year after his death, this *Outline* is of considerable value. The short but important paper, written at Christmas 1937, called *The Splitting of the Ego in the Process of Defence*, was also published in 1940. Freud maintained that it was wrong to think of the ego as a unitary synthesis, and that in early childhood splitting could take place. From this sprang further research and further theory, notably from Melanie Klein, and subsequently from many others. The concept of splitting is now a corner-stone in the understanding of schizophrenia.

In February Schur and Anna became convinced that there was a recurrence of the cancer. They wrote urgently to Pichler, who advised electrocoagulation, followed by radium. The director of the Curie Institute in Paris was fetched, but he could not advocate radium treatment. A biopsy disclosed unmistakable signs of malignancy, and the surgeons decided it was inaccessible. Only palliative treatment remained. Daily journeys to Harley Street for röntgen rays kept the trouble at bay, but proved exhausting.

In his last letter to Marie Bonaparte he wrote, 'The radium has once more begun to eat in and my world is again what it was before – a little island of pain floating on a sea of indifference'. It is to be doubted whether there is a more artistic and succinct description of advanced invalidism anywhere in literature.

Freud was so eager to see his *Moses* book appear in English before he died that Katherine Jones worked hard at the translation. It was published in March. He wrote to Hans Sachs, 'The *Moses* is not an unworthy leave-taking'.

In April Schur had to go to the United States to ensure his family's future. When he got back he found a great change in Freud's condition. Even his best friend, sound sleep, was now deserting him, and Anna had to apply orthoform locally several times each night.

One of Freud's last visitors was Hanns Sachs, who had been one of his first analytical friends. Sachs was especially struck by the courage of his 'master and friend' (the title of his book on Freud). Not only was he never irritable, but he took great interest in the American situation and appeared fully informed about the personalities and recent events in the analytical circles there. Their final parting was made in a friendly and unemotional fashion.

Like all good doctors, Freud was averse to taking drugs. 'I prefer to think in torment than not to be able to think clearly.' At last he consented to an occasional dose of aspirin. In August he became very weak and spent his time in a sick bay in his study, from where he could gaze at the flowers in the garden. He followed world events to the end – reading the newspapers, confident that the second world war would bring the end of Hitler. There was an air raid warning (a false alarm) on the day the war broke out, and Freud, lying on his couch in the garden, watched unperturbed the precautions taken to safeguard his manuscripts and antiques. A broadcast announced this was to be the last war, and Schur asked him if he believed that. Freud replied, 'Anyhow it is my last war.' It became impossible for him to eat anything. The last book he was able to read was Balzac's *La Peau de Chagrin*. He commented, 'That is just the book for me. It deals with starvation.' With all this agony, there was still no sign of impatience or anger – the acceptance of unalterable reality triumphed.

The cancer ate its way through the cheek and the septic condition grew worse. The exhaustion was extreme, the misery past description. On 19 September Jones was sent for to say goodbye. Freud opened his eyes, recognized him, waved his hand and then dropped it – a gesture expressing everything. On 21 September he said to Schur, 'You remember our first talk; you promised me that you would help me when I could no longer carry on. It is only torture now, and it no longer has any sense.' Schur pressed his hand and promised he would give adequate sedation. Freud thanked him and added, 'Tell Anna about our talk'.

Next morning Schur gave Freud a third of a grain of morphia. For any patient at such a point of exhaustion and so complete a stranger to opiates that small dose sufficed. He sighed with relief and sank into a peaceful sleep. It was evident that he was close to the end of his strength. He died just before midnight the next day – 23 September 1939. His long, arduous life was over, and he died as he had learnt to live – a realist.

A large number of mourners were present at the cremation at Golders Green. His ashes repose there in the favourite Grecian Urn. Jones delivered the funeral oration, and Stefan Zweig made a speech in German. But the understanding of the nature of man which Freud left to us continues; it is unlikely to be forgotten.

Definition of some Freudian terms

Conscious – Unconscious The *unconscious* mind has a separate existence from the *conscious*. It is the source of instinctive drives and contains all primary processes. These drives, which Freud designated the *id*, employ ruthless methods to achieve their ends. They are entirely concerned with self-preservation and physical appetites but, as an individual grows physically and matures psychologically, objects not immediately connected with food and sex take over some of the importance which these originally held. All memories both pleasurable and painful, are contained in the unconscious which – and this is a key point – is timeless.

Id is the Latin for 'that thing' and Freud employed this small word to mean the amalgamation of all instinctive activity.

Super-ego The *super-ego* can be thought of as the conscience, or as the civilizing agent in human beings. Contrary to expectation – and to the beliefs of many teachers – Freud found it to be largely unconscious, and that it was already formed by the end of the nursery years.

Ego Between the demands of the id and the strictures of the super-ego, Freud discerned a territory which he called the *ego*. The end aim of analysis, he said, was an ideal state: 'where Id was, there shall Ego be'. In this phrase he was stressing that insight into the unconscious, libidinal (id-based) demands and the subsequent conscious appraisal of them, lessens the tension that is liable to arise whenever the drives from the id become crushed by the super-ego.

Libido This word is used to denote the psychic energy which is employed to fulfil the instinctive drives situated in the id.

Conflict The unconscious has within it sets of emotions and phantasies which can be discrete and contradictory. These separate feelings can co-exist peacefully, but often they *conflict*. Unconscious conflicts only make themselves felt in the individual's conscious life by producing neurotic or psychotic symptoms of varying intensity. Some of these symptoms are common to mankind – slips of the tongue, the occasional forgetting of names or dates. Others, such as hysterical outbursts or paranoid delusions, must be regarded as serious symptoms.

Repression Freud used this word to describe the unconscious selection and suppression of memories, facts and ideas which could in some way be felt as connected with unpleasure.

Resistance The conscious mind is highly *resistant* to being informed about many of the contents of the unconscious.

Transference Any person who is helped, through the work of a psychoanalyst or psychotherapist, to overcome such a resistance may find himself at the mercy of violent and irrational feelings of love or hatred towards his helper. These reactions Freud named a *transference*, because he said they were feelings transferred from the patient's childhood. They were feelings such as would be more appropriate towards his parents, or to those who were first in charge of him when he was young.

Oedipus complex Certain experiences which take place during childhood have for each adult something of a nightmare or traumatic quality. Each such experience remains in the unconscious as a nucleus of complex feelings, fantasies and ideas. Freud formulated the *Oedipus complex* as a result of his realization that his patients' stories about being seduced when children were for the most part fabrications, the outcome of their wish thinking. Through his self-analysis and through listening to his patients, Freud was able to recover memories which he felt proved conclusively that small children love their parents in a manner which he could only term as sexual. He was sure that between the ages of three and six every child is in love with a parent or guardian of the opposite sex and fears the rivalry from someone of the same sex, more often than not the other parent.

Infant sexuality Freud began to demarcate the maturation of instinctive life not only by the study of children but by the careful treatment of patients with definite neuroses, and of those subjects who could be regarded as normal (for example, visiting doctors wanting to know more of Freud's methods). He considered that the infant during its first year and a half of life is concerned with *oral* needs, and with the person who is responsible for satisfying them. The following eighteen months or so he held to be the *anal* phase; at three years he found that children entered what he called the *genital* phase. From the age of five or six until puberty Freud thought that children went through a *latency* period where the insistent demands of the instincts were less urgent, intellectual stimuli beginning to predominate.

Identification The process of *identification* which continues through childhood is not, however, an intellectual process as is, say imitation, and should not be confused with it as such. Imitation is largely conscious and can account for many choices made by school children. Identification begins in babyhood and can continue throughout a lifetime. Usually a person identifies himself with those who were important to him, such as a parent, or a senior member of the family. Husbands and wives sometimes identify themselves with each other quite unconsciously, while pupils often identify more with those who teach them than they realize.

Chronological Table

This table traces very roughly some of the main turning-points in Freud's intellectual development and opinions. A few of the chief events in his external life are also included.

1856 6 May. Born at Freiberg in Moravia.
1860 Family settle in Vienna.
1865 Enters Gymnasium (secondary school).
1873 Enters Vienna University as medical student.
1876–82 Works under Brücke at the Institute of Physiology in Vienna.
1877 First publications: papers on anatomy and physiology.
1881 Graduates as Doctor of Medicine.
1882 Engagement to Martha Bernays.
1882–5 Works in Vienna General Hospital, concentrating on cerebral anatomy; numerous publications.
1884–7 Researches into the clinical uses of cocaine.
1885 Appointed *Privatdozent* (University lecturer) in Neuropathology.
1885 (October)–1886 (February) Studies under Charcot at the Salpêtrière Hospital for Nervous Diseases in Paris. Interest first turns to hysteria and hypnosis.
1886 Marriage to Martha Bernays. Sets up private practice in nervous diseases in Vienna.
1886–93 Continues work on neurology, especially on the cerebral palsies of children at the Kassowitz Institute in Vienna, with numerous publications. Gradual shift of interest from neurology to psychopathology.
1887 Birth of eldest child (Mathilde).
1887–1901 Friendship and correspondence with Wilhelm Fliess in Berlin. Freud's letters to him during this period, published posthumously in 1950, throw much light on the development of his views.

1887   Begins the use of hypnotic suggestion in his practice.

c. 1888 Begins to follow Breuer in using hypnosis for cathartic treatment of hysteria. Gradually drops hypnosis and substitutes free association.

1889   Visits Bernheim at Nancy to study his suggestion technique.

1889   Birth of eldest son (Martin).

1891   Monograph on *Aphasia*. Birth of second son (Oliver).

1892   Birth of youngest son (Ernst).

1893   Publication of Breuer and Freud's *Preliminary Communication*: exposition of trauma theory of hysteria and of cathartic treatment.
Birth of second daughter (Sophie).

1893-8 Researches and short papers on hysteria, obsessions, and anxiety.

1895   Publication of *Studies on Hysteria*, written in conjunction with Breuer: case histories and description by Freud on his technique, including first account of transference.

1893-6 Gradual divergence of views between Freud and Breuer. Freud introduces concepts of defence and repression and of neurosis being a result of a conflict between the ego and the libido.

1895   *Project for a Scientific Psychology*: included in Freud's letters to Fliess and first published in 1950. An abortive attempt to state psychology in neurological terms, but foreshadows much of Freud's later theories. Birth of youngest child (Anna).

1896   Introduces the term 'psychoanalysis'. Death of father (aged eighty).

1897   Freud's self-analysis, leading to the abandonment of the trauma theory and the recognition of infantile sexuality and the Oedipus complex.

1900   *The Psychopathology of Everyday Life*. This, together with the book on dreams, made it plain that Freud's theories applied not only to pathological states but also to normal mental life.

1902   Appointed Professor Extraordinarius.

1905 *Three Essays on the Theory of Sexuality*: tracing for the first time the course of development of the sexual instinct in human beings from infancy to maturity.

c. 1906 Jung becomes an adherent of psychoanalysis.

1908 First international meeting of psychoanalysts (at Salzburg).

1909 Freud and Jung invited to the USA to lecture. Case history of the first analysis of a child (Little Hans, aged five): confirming inferences previously made from adult analyses, especially as to infantile sexuality and the Oedipus and castration complexes.

c. 1910 First emergence of the theory of 'narcissism'.

1911 Secession of Adler.

1911–15 Papers on the technique of psychoanalysis.
Application of psychoanalytic theories to a psychotic case.

1913–14 *Totem and Taboo*: application of psychoanalysis to anthropological material.

1914 Secession of Jung.
On the History of the Psycho-Analytic Movement: includes a polemical section on Adler and Jung. Writes his last major case history, of the 'Wolf Man' (not published till 1918).

1915 Writes a series of twelve 'metapsychological' papers on basic theoretical questions, of which only five have survived.

1915–17 *Introductory Lectures*: giving an extensive general account of the state of Freud's views up to the time of the First World War.

1919 Application of the theory of narcissism to the war neuroses.

1920 Death of second daughter.
Beyond the Pleasure Principle: the first explicit introduction of the concept of the 'compulsion to repeat' and of the theory of the 'death instinct'.

1921 *Group Psychology*: beginnings of a systematic analytic study of the ego.

1923 *The Ego and the Id*: revised account of the structure and functioning of the mind with the division into an id, an ego, and a super-ego.

1923 First onset of cancer.

1925 Revised views on the sexual development of women.

1926 *Inhibitions, Symptoms and Anxiety*: revised views on the problem of anxiety.

1927 *The Future of an Illusion*: a discussion of religion.

1930 *Civilisation and its Discontents*.
Freud awarded the Goethe Prize by the City of Frankfurt.
Death of mother (aged ninety-five).

1933 Hitler seizes power in Germany; Freud's books publicly burned in Berlin.

1934–8 *Moses and Monotheism*: the last of Freud's works to appear during his lifetime.

1936 Eightieth birthday. Election as Corresponding Member of Royal Society.

1938 Hitler's invasion of Austria. Freud leaves Vienna for London.
An Outline of Psycho-Analysis. A final, unfinished, but profound exposition of psychoanalysis.

1939 23 September. Death in London.

The main works of Sigmund Freud

Dates of lectures delivered or works written

1891   *On Aphasia* Imago Publishing Co. London, 1953

1893   'On the Psychical Mechanism of Hysterical Phenomena: Preliminary Communication' Studies on Hysteria with Breuer J.

1895   *Studies on Hysteria* London, with Breuer, J. Hogarth Press, 1956

1900   *The Interpretation of Dreams* London, Allen and Unwin, 1955

1901   *The Psychopathology of Everyday Life* Standard Edition, Vol VI

1905   *Jokes and Their Relation to the Unconscious* London, Routledge and Kegan Paul, 1960

1905   *Three Essays on the Theory of Sexuality* London, Hogarth Press, 1962

1909   'Analysis of a Phobia in a Five-year old Boy' in Standard Edition, Vol. X

1910   'Contributions to the Psychology of Love' Vol. I in Standard Edition, Vol. XIV

1910   'Experiences Concerning the Psychic Life of the Child' in *Collected Papers on Analytic Psychology* London, Baillière, Tindall and Cox, 1916

1911   'Psycho-Analytic Notes on a Case of Paranoia' (with Dr. Schreber)

1912–13   *Totem and Taboo* London, Routledge and Kegan Paul, 1950

1914   'On the History of the Psycho-Analytic Movement' in Standard Edition, Vol. XIV

1916–17   *Introductory Lectures on Psycho-Analysis* London, Allen and Unwin, 1929

1918   'From the History of an Infantile Neurosis ('The Wolf Man') in Standard Edition, Vol. XVII

1920   *Beyond the Pleasure Principle* London, Hogarth Press, 1961

1921   *Group Psychology and the Analysis of the Ego* London, Hogarth Press, 1959

✓ 1923   *The Ego and the Id* London, Hogarth Press, 1961

1925   'Josef Breuer (Obituary)' in Standard Edition Vol. XIX

✓ 1926   *Inhibitions, Symptoms and Anxiety* London, Hogarth Press, 1961

1927   *The Future of an Illusion* London, Hogarth Press

1930   *Civilisation and its Discontents* London, Hogarth Press

1939   *Moses and Monotheism* London, Hogarth Press, 1939

1939   *An Outline of Psycho-Analysis* London, Hogarth Press, 1949

1895   *The Origins of Psycho-Analysis* (includes 'A Project for a Scientific Psychology', 1895) London, Hogarth Press, 1954

1873–1939   *Letters* (1873–1939) edited by Ernst Freud London, Hogarth Press, 1961

Further reading

Jones, Ernest, *Sigmund Freud, Life and Work* (3 Vols), London, Hogarth Press 1958

Psychoanalysis
Brown, J. A. C., *Freud and the Post-Freudians*, Penguin Books, Harmondsworth 1961

Fenichel, O., *The Psychoanalytic Theory of Neurosis*, Routledge and Kegan Paul, London 1966

Erikson, E. H., *Childhood and Society*, Penguin Books, Harmondsworth 1967

Bowlby, J., *Child Care and the Growth of Love*, Penguin Books, Harmondsworth 1963

Jung, C. G. (Ed), *Studies in Word-Association*, London, Heinemann, 1918

Laing, R. D., *The Divided Self*, Penguin Books, Harmondsworth 1967

Klein, M., *Envy and Gratitude*, Tavistock Publications Ltd, London 1957

Storr, A., *The Integrity of the Personality*, Penguin Books, Harmondsworth 1963

Winnicott, D. W., *The Child, the Family and the Outside World*, Penguin Books, Harmondsworth 1963

The Family and Individual Development, Tavistock Publications Ltd, London 1965

Sharpe, Ella, *Dream Analysis*, Hogarth Press, 1937

Suttie, J., *The Origins of Love and Hate*, Penguin Books, Harmondsworth

Klein, M. and Others, *Love, Hate and Reparation*, Hogarth Press

Psychology

Bromley, D. B., *The Psychology of Human Ageing*, Penguin Books, Harmondsworth 1966

Eysenck, H. J., *Fact and Fiction in Psychology*, Penguin Books, Harmondsworth 1965

Lazarus, R. S. and Opton, E. M. (Eds), *Personality*, Penguin Books, Harmondsworth 1967

Masters, W. H. and Johnson V. E., *Human Sexual Inadequacy*, Churchill Ltd, London 1970
Human Sexual Response, Little, Brown, Boston 1966

Sandström, C. I., *The Psychology of Childhood and Adolescence*, Penguin Books, Harmondsworth 1966

Wright, D. S. etc., *Introducing Psychology: an experimental approach*, Penguin Books, Harmondsworth 1970

Ethology

Ardrey, R., *The Territorial Imperative*, Collins, Sons and Co., Ltd, London 1967

Lorenz, K., *On Aggression*, Methuen and Co., Ltd, London 1963

Morris, D., *The Naked Ape*, Cape, London 1967

Psychiatry

Fish, F., *Outline of Psychiatry*, Wright and Sons Ltd, Bristol 1964

Soddy, K., *Clinical Child Psychiatry*, Ballière, Tindall and Cassell, Ltd, London 1960

Stafford-Clark, D., *Psychiatry Today*, Penguin Books, Harmondsworth 1966

Sociology

Newson, J. and E., *Four Years Old in an Urban Community*, Allen and Unwin Ltd., 1968
Patterns of Infant Care in an Urban Community, Penguin Books, Harmondsworth 1965

Gavron, H., *The Captive Wife – Conflicts of Housebound Mothers*, Penguin Books, Harmondsworth 1966

Townsend, P., *The Family Life of Old People*, Penguin
Books, Harmondsworth 1963
Willmott, P., *Adolescent Boys of East London*, Penguin
Books, Harmondsworth 1966
Young, M. and Willmott, P., *Family and Kinship in East
London*, Penguin Books, Harmondsworth 1967

Social Psychology
Allport, G. W., *Pattern and Growth in Personality*, Holt,
Rinehart and Winston, London 1969
Argyle, M., *The Psychology of Interpersonal Behaviour*,
Penguin Books, Harmondsworth 1967
Berne, E., *Games People Play*, Andre Deutsch, London
1966 and Penguin Books, Harmondsworth 1968 (ppb)
Lindgren, H. C., *Introduction to Social Psychology*, John
Wiley and Sons Ltd, London and New York 1969
Ruddock, R., *Roles and Relationships*, Routledge and
Kegan Paul, London 1969

Social Casework
Younghusband, E. (Ed), *New Developments in Casework*,
Allen and Unwin, London 1968

Index